D0597585

MILNER CRAFT SERIES

Stumpwork Embroidery Designs and Projects

Jane Nicholas

SALLY MILNER PUBLISHING

To John - with love.

First published in 1998 by
Sally Milner Publishing Pty Ltd
RMB 54 Burra Road
Burra Creek 2620
New South Wales
Australia

© Jane Nicholas, 1998

Design by Anna Warren, Warren Ventures, Sydney
Photography by Andrew Elton, Sydney
Printed in Hong Kong
Endpaper picture of an Elizabethan pillowcover courtesy of the
Trustees of the Victoria and Albert Museum, London

National Library of Australia Cataloguing-in-Publication data:
    Nicholas, Jane.
    Stumpwork embroidery : designs & projects.

    Includes index.
    ISBN 1 86351 208 4

    1. Stumpwork. I. Title. (Series : Milner craft series).

    746.44

All rights reserved. No part of this publication may be reproduced, stored in a retrieval system or transmitted in any form or by any means, electronic, mechanical, photocopying, recording or other-wise, without prior written permission of the copyright holders.

Contents

Acknowledgements

I would like to extend my sincere thanks to all the people who have shared their passion for stumpwork with me. Whether by letter or in class, your enthusiasm has been an inspiration, and is the raison d'être for this book.

My adventures with stumpwork would not have been possible without the love and encouragement of my family — John, Joanna, Katie and David. I am indebted to my husband, John, for his patience, versatility and sense of humour!

My special thanks to my 'sewing friends' for their support, particularly to Judy MacMaster for being there, whatever the need.

I am especially grateful to Janice, for keeping my life in order, and to our loyal staff at Chelsea — Kim, Jenny and Ginnie.

Lastly, to my publisher and editor, Sally Milner, and designer Anna Warren — your expertise is greatly appreciated.

JANE NICHOLAS, 1998

Introduction

Stumpwork is a modern term used to refer to a particular form of raised embroidery, popular in England during the second half of the seventeenth century, when it was regarded as the culmination of the needlework education for young girls from wealthy Stuart households. Usually stitched on an ivory satin background with silk and gold threads, these embroideries contained a myriad of fruits, flowers, insects, animals and people, with no regard to size, scale or perspective! The motifs were often padded to give dimension, or pieces were embroidered separately then applied as raised, detached shapes, such as flower petals. The work might then be embellished, with beads, shells, feathers and spangles, all of which must have given as much pleasure then as it is giving embroiderers more than 300 years later.

Stumpwork embroidery is enjoying a vigorous revival which is showing no signs of abating. Rather than copying the past, a variety of interpretations of raised embroidery has evolved, from the emphasis on needlelace in the UK, to the political overtones of the arpilleras of Chile and Peru. Patchworkers are including raised pieces in their Baltimore quilts and Brazilian embroiderers are blending both techniques. The response to my first book on stumpwork has been overwhelming. I have received letters of shared enthusiasm from all around the world, revealing an amazing network of people sharing a common passion. It has been very exciting!

I am still teaching in Sydney and Bowral, travel to all States regularly, and have had wonderful adventures in the United States, Canada and New Zealand. These classes have inspired me to develop new designs and ideas, resulting in a collection of more than 30 projects, half of which are in my first book. This new book could well have been titled The Other Half. It contains the designs and instructions for 19 projects and 28 new motifs and is divided into five sections.

The Field Flowers section contains the first three in a series on wildflowers — a fascinating and ongoing study, not only of the history of the plants but also the folk lore associated with them. Pansies with detached petals were first introduced in the Mirror Frame but I have found them addictive — every time I see a new pansy I find my mind searching for threads to replicate them. I share seven colour-ways here but you can substitute your own for these charming cottage flowers. The scrolling floral designs found on garments and furnishings in the Elizabethan period is another area of interest, providing the inspiration for the Roundels which were worked for the EGA Seminar '96 in San Francisco. Animals and birds were favourite subjects in traditional stumpwork; a deer, owl and parrot have been included here, but the techniques can be used to interpret many other animals that you may wish to capture in your work. The Needlework Accessories were designed in response to a request to develop pieces in stumpwork that had a practical application. Incorporating motifs from both books, these were great fun to make and would be lovely gifts for special friends.

I hope that this book may be just that — a gift for special embroiderers who share my love for stumpwork. It has been very satisfying to collect everything together (even my name brooch) and record it all — rather like spring cleaning or tidying your sewing basket. I look forward to working on the new projects that jostle for attention in my ideas diary — stumpwork has so much potential! Embroiderers need never lack for subject matter, given the constant inspiration from nature and all the decorative arts.

Nature doth teach us all to have aspiring minds.

CHRISTOPHER MARLOWE (1564-1593)

I consider myself to be incredibly blessed to have these opportunities to meet with like-minded people and share the joy of a new idea.

Jane Nicholas, 1998

How to Use This Book

Before you begin it is important that you read the following information:

• It is assumed that the embroiderer has access to the first book, (*Stumpwork Embroidery — A Collection of Fruits, Flowers and Insects for Contemporary Raised Embroidery*), for information on all the materials and equipment used in stumpwork, and for detailed instructions on all the basic stumpwork techniques. Some of the designs contain elements from this book. Any reference to the first book is marked ✸.

• The diagrams accompanying the instructions for the projects are accurate in size unless otherwise specified. However, the explanatory drawings accompanying the individual motifs may not be true to scale.

• The transferring of designs is done with tracing paper (GLAD Bake) and lead pencil (see p. 28 ✸) unless otherwise specified. When tracing on to a light coloured background, use a minimum amount of lead.

• DMC threads are used throughout the book unless otherwise indicated. Occasionally other threads are used, and a chart comparing them to a DMC equivalent is on page 189.

• The majority of stitching is done with one strand of thread in a fine (10) crewel/embroidery needle. Select the needle size according to the number (or thickness) of threads being used.

• Many of the designs can be used for surface embroidery without the raised components.

The stumpwork embroiderer's workbox should contain the following equipment:

- Good quality embroidery hoops — 7 cm, 10 cm, 15 cm, 23 cm (3", 4", 6", 9")

- Needles: Crewel/Embroidery (sizes 3—10)
  Straw/Milliners (sizes 1—10)
  Sharps (sizes 10—12)
  Tapestry (sizes 24—26)
  Chenille (sizes 18—24)
  Yarn Darners (size 14)

- Scissors — small, with sharp points

- Thimble

- Pins — fine glass-headed pins

- Wire cutters

- Screwdriver (for tightening the embroidery hoop)

- Tweezers (fine — from medical suppliers)

- Eyebrow comb (for Turkey knots)

- Ideas diary and pencil

GLOSSARY OF PRODUCT NAMES

This list gives equivalent names for products used throughout this book and which may not be available under the same name in every country.

PRODUCT	EQUIVALENT
Vilene	non-woven interfacing
GLAD Bake	baking parchment
Drawing pins	thumb tacks
Calico	muslin
Clutch pencil	mechanical pencil
Biro	ballpoint pen

Field Flowers

Ye field flowers! the gardens eclipse you, 'tis true:

Yet, wildings of nature! I dote upon you.

For ye waft me to summers of old,

When the earth teemed around me with fairy delight,

And when daisies and buttercups gladdened my sight

Like treasures of silver and gold.

THOMAS CAMPBELL FIELD FLOWERS (1774-1844)

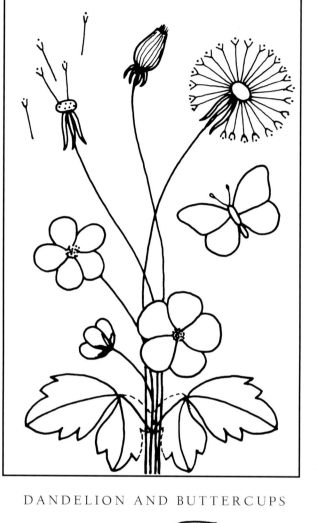

DANDELION AND BUTTERCUPS

Skeleton outline

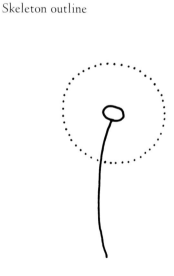

Detached leaves

Buttercup
large petal

Medium petal

Buttercup
bud petal

Blue Butterfly
front wing

Blue Butterfly
back wing

Dandelion
seedhead guide

Dandelion and Buttercups

REQUIREMENTS

- Ivory satin (or fabric of choice) — 28 cm x 28 cm (11'' x 11'')

- Calico (or quilter's muslin) for backing —28 cm x 28 cm (11'' x 11'')

- 20 cm or 23 cm (8'' or 9'') embroidery hoop

- 'Blue' butterfly (see p.21)

- Buttercups (see p.14)

- Dandelion (see p.17)

ORDER OF WORK

1. Mount the main fabric and the backing fabric into the embroidery hoop.

2. Trace the skeleton outline onto the main fabric.

3. Buttercup stems.

4. Dandelion stems, bud and seed heads.

5. Butterfly.

6. Buttercups.

7. Detached buttercup leaves.

BUTTERCUPS

Buttercups or gold of the meadow are the gold-cups and cuckoo-buds of Shakespeare:

And cuckoo-buds of yellow hue
Do paint the meadows with delight.

Many children are introduced to the glossy yellow flower by having a blossom held beneath their chin the yellow reflection on the skin indicating that they love butter!

MATERIALS REQUIRED

- Calico (or quilter's muslin) 2 x (20 cm x 20 cm) (8'' x 8'')

- 10 cm (4'') and 15 cm (6'') embroidery hoops

- Wire: Fine flower wire, cut in 12 cm (5'') lengths
  30 gauge green covered, cut in 18 cm (7'') lengths

- Yellow marking pen to colour wire (optional)

- Fine tweezers to shape wire

- Needles: Crewel/embroidery 5-10
  Straw/milliners 3-9
  Chenille 18

- Thread: Dark yellow stranded thread (Cifonda 1116 or DMC 725)
  Medium yellow stranded thread (Cifonda 1115 or DMC 726)
  Pale green stranded thread (DMC 3819)
  Medium green stranded thread (DMC 469)
  Lighter green stranded thread (DMC 470)

Buttercup stems and detached leaves

1.   Work the stems in chain stitch with three strands of mixed green threads (2 x 470, 1 x 469)

2.   Work two pairs of detached leaves, on calico/muslin mounted in a hoop, as follows:
— couch then overcast the green wire down the central vein (470)
— couch then buttonhole the wire around the outside edge (469)
— work the side veins with stem stitch (470)
— embroider the leaf surface in straight stitches (469).

3.   Cut out and apply a pair of leaves to the ends of both leaf stems, using the chenille needle to insert the wires through to the back of the work. Secure then trim the wires.

Buttercup flowers

1.   Mount the calico/muslin into a 15 cm (6'') hoop and trace five large and five medium petals. Colour the flower wire with marking pen if desired. The petals are embroidered with one strand of thread.

2.   Using the dark yellow thread (1116 or 725), couch the wire to the calico around each petal shape leaving two tails of wire at the base of the petal, then stitch the wire to the calico with small, close buttonhole stitches, incorporating the couching stitches and working the buttonhole ridge on the outside edge of the petal.

   Using the same thread, embroider the top third of each petal with a row of long and short buttonhole stitch, worked close together and close to the inside edge of the wire. Keep the stitch direction towards the centre of the buttercup.

   Work the remainder of the petal in straight stitches with medium yellow thread (1115 or 726), keeping the stitch direction towards the centre of the petal.

3.   Using sharp scissors, cut out the petals close to the buttonholed edge, avoiding the wire tails. The buttercup petals are attached to the main fabric by inserting the wire tails

Large petal

Medium petal

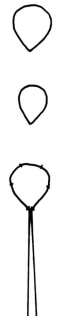

through five holes in a circle (very close together) using a large chenille needle. Secure each petal by separating the wires and stitching to the back of the work, then bend the wire back and stitch again. Trim the wires. It is easier to secure each petal before proceeding to the next.

4. Work the centre of each buttercup with French knots (two strands, one wrap) with a straw needle in pale green thread (3819). Carefully shape the petals with tweezers.

Buttercup bud

1. To work three detached bud petals, mount calico/muslin into a hoop and trace three bud shapes. With one strand of dark yellow thread (1116 or 725), couch then buttonhole the wire to the calico around the outside edge of each petal. Leave two tails of wire for the centre petal, and one tail for the two side petals.

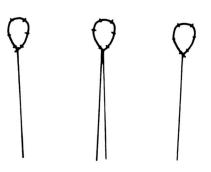

Work long and short buttonhole stitch inside the wire with medium yellow thread (1115 or 726). Add a few straight stitches at the base of the bud petals in pale green (3819).

2. Embroider two bud petals on the main fabric. Work the top edges of the petals in long and short buttonhole stitch in dark yellow thread (1116 or 725) then the remainder of the petal in straight stitches in medium yellow thread (1115 or 726).

3. The detached bud petals are applied to the main fabric, at the base of the embroidered petals, by inserting all the wire tails through one hole using a large chenille needle. Apply the two side petals first, then the centre petal. Secure each petal with small stitches at the back of the work.

4. Carefully shape the bud petals with tweezers then work four sepals with detached chain stitches, (through to the back of the work), with two strands of green thread (470). Take care not to flatten the petals when stitching through them.

DANDELION

The dandelion is a plant that is worth careful observation, for its life history abounds in interesting events. As a typical example of dandelion behaviour, watch the development of one single flower-head. At first the stalk is erect, holding up its bright yellow blossom, rich in nectar, for every insect to see. When the seeds have been fertilised, however, the blossom closes tightly, and the stalk lies down out of the way. Finally, when the seeds are ripe, the stalk rises to the vertical again. It has grown much longer during its retirement, and so is able to hoist its globular mass of silken parachutes high into the air.

RICHARD MORSE, THE BOOK OF WILDFLOWERS

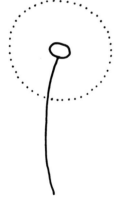

Dandelion
seedhead guide

In the language of flowers, dandelion means oracle, originating from the superstition that if you blow off all the seeds on the seedhead in one breath, your wish will come true. The name dandelion comes from the French *dent-de-lion*, for the jagged leaves resemble the teeth of a lion.

MATERIALS REQUIRED

- Beige felt and paper-backed fusible web 5 cm x 8 cm (3'' x 2'')
- Masking tape
- Tracing paper and silk tacking/basting thread

- Needles: Crewel/embroidery 5-10
  Sharps 10 (or 12 Appliqué)
  Chenille 18
  Tapestry 26

- Thread: Dark mauve/plum stranded (Au Ver à Soie d'Alger 4645 or DMC 3726)
  Medium mauve/plum stranded (Au Ver à Soie d'Alger 4644 or DMC 316)
  Pale mauve/plum stranded (Au Ver à Soie d'Alger 4643 or DMC 778)
  Dark khaki green stranded (Au Ver à Soie d'Alger 2134 or DMC 3011)
  Medium khaki green stranded (Au Ver à Soie d'Alger 2132 or DMC 3012)
  Beige fine silk stranded (Cifonda Silk 496)
  Mauve soft cotton thread for padding (DMC Tapestry Cotton 2113)

Dandelion stems

The stems are worked in Raised Stem Stitch Band over a padding of soft cotton thread.

1. To pad the stem, place one length of soft cotton thread along the stem line inserting the ends through to the back at the base and top of this line with the chenille needle. Temporarily secure the ends of the soft cotton with masking tape — trim away when the stem is worked.

2. Couch the padding in place with stitches about 4 mm (³⁄₈'') apart using one strand of thread in a crewel needle. To ensure a rounded raised stem, enter and exit each couching stitch from the same hole on the traced stem line, taking care not to pierce the padding thread.

3. To embroider the stem, cover the padding with four rows of stem stitch worked over these couching stitches. All the rows of stem stitch are worked in the same direction, each row entering and exiting at the same points as the padding thread. Changing colours where indicated, work with one strand of thread in a tapestry needle so as not to pierce the padding thread.

Cross-section of couching

padding thread

couching thread

fabric

Embroider the stems in the following order, working the rows of raised stem stitch in the colours and sequence indicated.

(A) SPENT DANDELION STEM:

— couch in medium green thread (2132 or 3012)

— rows of stem stitch —pale mauve/medium green/medium green/medium green.

(B) CLOSED DANDELION BUD STEM:

— couch in medium mauve/plum thread (4644 or 316)

— rows of stem stitch — dark mauve/medium mauve/medium mauve/pale mauve.

(C) OPEN DANDELION STEM:
(*Worked over all other stems*)

— couch in pale mauve thread (4643 or 778)

— rows of stem stitch — medium mauve/pale mauve/pale mauve/medium green.

Closed dandelion bud

1.   Using the paper-backed fusible web, cut three pieces of felt to pad the bud, one the actual size of the bud and two successively smaller.

2.   With one strand of dark green thread (2134 or 3011), stab stitch the smaller layers in place, then apply and outline the larger shape with buttonhole stitch, leaving the top edge open.

3.   Using the same thread, embroider the felt with rows of chain stitch (not too tight), staggering the starting point of every alternate row to achieve the effect of closed sepals around the bud. To prevent flattening the shape, most stitches are scooped through the top layer of felt, working loose stitches at the open top edge of the bud.

4.   Using two strands of beige silk thread (496) work long loops into the bud through the open top end, securing at the back of the work when necessary. Trim the loops close to the top edge of the bud to give the effect of fluffy seed heads about to burst open.

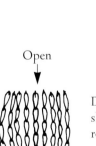

Open

Diagram of bud showing staggered rows of chain stitch

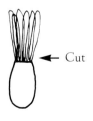

← Cut

5. Work three small sepals (5 mm or ¼" long) in needleweaving at the base of the bud with one strand of medium green thread in the tapestry needle (See Stitch Glossary).

Open dandelion seedhead

1. Outline the base in backstitch with one strand of medium green thread (2132 or 3012), then cover with padded satin stitch.

2. Using the same thread in a tapestry needle, work three long sepals (1 cm or ⅜") in needleweaving under the base.

3. Cut the seedhead guide out of tracing paper, hold over the stem and base and use as a template to stitch around with small running stitches in silk tacking/basting thread.

4. Using the tacking/basting as a guide, work long fly stitches around the satin stitched base with one strand of beige silk thread (496) in a sharps needle. Remove the tacking/basting then embroider French knots in the space above each fly stitch.

Spent dandelion seedhead

1. Outline the base in backstitch with one strand of medium green thread (2132 or 3012), then cover with padded satin stitch.

2. Using the same thread in a tapestry needle, work three long sepals (1 cm or ⅜") in needleweaving under the base (See Stitch Glossary).

3. Work small dots (one stitch) with one strand of dark green thread (2134 or 3011).

4. With one strand of beige silk thread (496), work a long fly stitch with a small split stitch at the base and a French knot at the top for each seedhead. Place them at random — some attached to the base, others scattered.

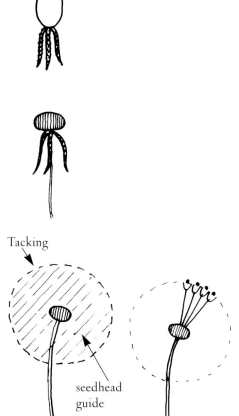

Tacking

seedhead guide

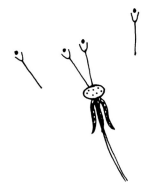

BLUE BUTTERFLY

The butterfly family Lycaenidae is found throughout the world and comprises several thousand small to medium-sized species. Most species have metallic upper side colouring, often shades of blue (the blues) but sometimes coppery orange-red (the coppers). The undersides are typically spotted or streaked in intricate patterns.

MATERIALS REQUIRED:

· Calico (or quilter's muslin) 20 cm x 20 cm (8'' x 8'')

· 10 cm (4'') embroidery hoop

· Wire: 30 gauge white covered or fine flower wire, cut in 12 cm (5'') lengths

· Fine tweezers to shape wire

· Needles: Crewel 10
Straw 1 and 9
Chenille 18

· Threads: Medium grey stranded silk (Cifonda 214)
Pale grey stranded silk (Cifonda 212)
Pale blue stranded silk (Cifonda 181)
Copper stranded silk (Cifonda 102)
Dark grey stranded silk (Madeira 1714)
Black/multi metallic machine (Madeira Metallic No.40 colour 270)
Copper metallic machine (Madeira Metallic No.40 colour 28)
Slate/black metallic (Kreinik Cord 225c)
Dark blue/brown variegated chenille (hunter/olive colour)

To embroider detached wings

1. Mount the calico/muslin into the hoop and trace two front and two back wings. The wings are embroidered with one strand of thread using the colours as indicated on the diagrams.

Front wing

Back wing

2. Couch, then buttonhole the wire to the calico around the wing outline, leaving a tail of wire at each end. Work buttonhole stitch in two colours, as shown, for front wing and one colour for back wing.

3. Work a row of long buttonhole stitches inside the wire to fill the outer edge of the wing.

4. Embroider the remainder of the wing with four rows of straight stitches blending into each other (encroaching satin stitch), blending the first row into the long buttonhole stitches.

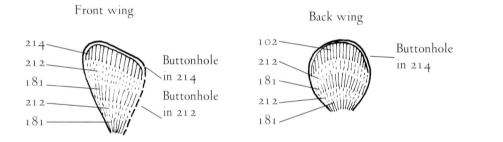

Front wing

214
212
181
212
181

Buttonhole in 214

Buttonhole in 212

Back wing

102
212
181
212
181

Buttonhole in 214

Wing Colours

5. With one strand of black/multi metallic thread in the small straw needle, work the veins of the wing in fly stitch and buttonhole stitch, using the diagram as a guide. Embroider the spots where desired with one strand of copper metallic thread.

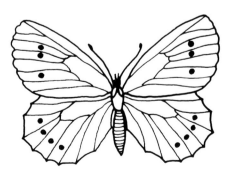

Veins of typical Blue Butterfly

Front wing veins showing direction of stitches

Back wing veins

To assemble and complete butterfly

1.   Make another dot between the two upper dots already marked on the fabric (now three dots for wings) — the lower dot indicates the length of the abdomen. Carefully cut out the wings and apply (back wings first) by inserting the wires through the three upper dots as shown, using the chenille needle. Secure the wires to the back of the work with tiny stitches. Trim the wires.

2.   To form the thorax, cover where the wings join with one stitch of the chenille thread.

3.   Work one bullion knot for the abdomen using eight strands of thread (4 x 214 and 4 x 1714) in the large straw needle, with as many wraps as necessary. Using the same thread, work a French knot (1 wrap) for the head.

4.   To work the antennae, make a small chain stitch for the knob with long tie-down stitch to the head, using the slate/black metallic thread in the small straw needle.

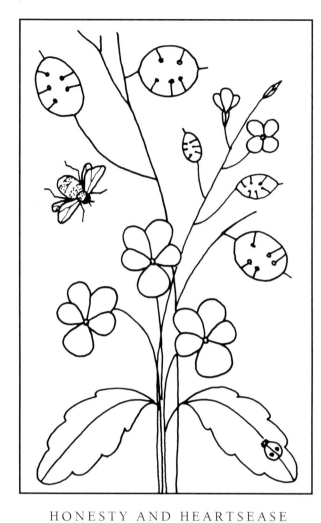

HONESTY AND HEARTSEASE

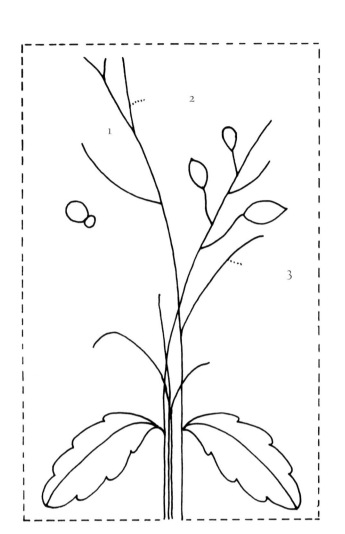

Skeleton outline

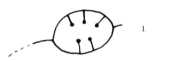

1

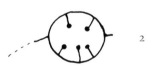

2

3

Dried honesty seed cases

Heartsease petals

1 and 2

3 and 4

Tiny ladybird

Buff-tailed bumble bee wings

Honesty flower petal

5

Honesty and Heartsease

REQUIREMENTS

- Ivory satin (or fabric of choice) — 28 cm x 28 cm (11'' x 11'')

- Calico (or quilter's muslin) for backing — 28 cm x 28 cm (11'' x 11'')

- 20 cm or 22 cm (8'' or 9'') embroidery hoop

- Buff-tailed bumble bee (see p. 34)

- Honesty (see p. 26)

- Heartsease (see p. 30)

- Tiny ladybird (see p. 37)

ORDER OF WORK

1. Mount the main fabric and the backing fabric into the embroidery hoop.

2. Trace the skeleton outline onto the main fabric. Do not trace the dotted lines indicating the position of the dried honesty seed cases.

3. Honesty stems, green seed pods and bud.

4. Heartsease stems and surface leaves.

5. Buff-tailed bumble bee.

6. Honesty flowers.

7. Dried honesty seed cases.

8. Heartsease flowers.

9. Detached heartsease leaves and ladybird.

HONESTY

Honesty or Lunaria is named after the moon because its luminescent seed pods reflect the moonlight and in medieval times it was thought to have many occult powers. When the cases of the dried seed pods are removed, the inner membranes glow transparently in the light. This see-through nature of the plant may account for it being called honesty.

MATERIALS REQUIRED

- Honey-coloured sparkle mottled organza — 15 cm x 15 cm (6'' x 6'')

- Cream rayon lining fabric — 15 cm x 15 cm (6'' x 6'')

- Paper-backed fusible web — 15 cm x 15 cm (6'' x 6'')

- Calico (or quilter's muslin) — 20 cm x 20 cm (8'' x 8'')

- 10 cm (4'') embroidery hoop

- Wire: 28 gauge uncovered (cut in 12 cm (5'') lengths)
  Fine flower wire (cut in 12 cm (5'') lengths)

- Purple marking pen to colour flower wire (optional)

- Fine tweezers to shape wire

- Needles: Crewel/embroidery or sharps 5-10
  Sharp yarn darner 14

- Threads: Honey-coloured stranded thread — DMC 738
  Honey-coloured rayon machine thread — Madeira Rayon
  No.40 colour1055
  Purple stranded thread — Cifonda 123 or DMC 552

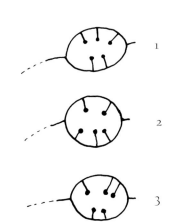

Dried honesty seed cases

Pale yellow stranded thread — DMC 744
Medium green stranded thread — DMC 3346
Light green stranded thread — DMC 3347

Honesty stems and seed pods

1.   The stems are worked in stem stitch with both shades of green in the needle. Start at the base with three strands of thread, then decrease to two strands to make the upper stems thinner.

2.   With one strand of 3347, embroider the seed pods with vertical satin stitches. With one strand of 3346, work the seed pod outline and point in back stitch, then work five or six straight stitches over the satin stitches for seed stalks.

Honesty flowers

1.   Mount the calico/muslin in the hoop and trace seven flower petals. Using one strand of purple thread, couch the flower wire to the fabric around each petal; six petals with one tail of wire, one petal (for the closed flower) with two tails of wire (see diagram). Work buttonhole stitch over the wire (and through the calico), incorporating the couching stitches. Embroider each petal inside the wire in long and short buttonhole stitch and straight stitches. Carefully cut out the petals.

2.   *Open honesty flower.* Use a large needle to make four holes, in which to insert the wire tails of four petals, close together around a central point at the end of the stem. Bend the wires underneath each petal and secure to the back of the work with tiny stitches. Trim the wires. Work four small French knots, with two strands of pale yellow thread, to form the centre of the flower. Shape the petals with tweezers.

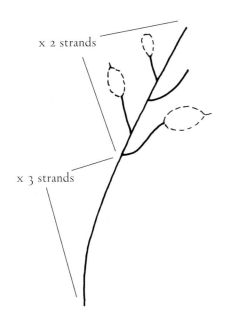

x 2 strands

x 3 strands

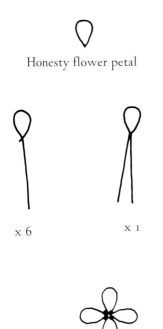

Honesty flower petal

x 6   x 1

3.   *Closed honesty flower.* Embroider the edge of the petal on the main fabric with long and short buttonhole stitch then fill with straight stitches. Apply the two side petals by inserting both wires through one hole at the base of the petal on the main fabric, then insert the petal with two wire tails through the same hole and secure all wires to the back of the work with tiny stitches. Carefully embroider three sepals through the detached petals, with single chain stitches in two strands of mixed green threads.

Honesty flower bud

1.   Work the bud at the end of the stem with straight stitches in one strand of purple thread.

2.   Embroider the sepals with single chain stitches in two strands of mixed green threads.

Dried honesty stems

The stems are worked in stem stitch with honey-coloured stranded thread (738). Start at the base with three strands of thread, then decrease to two strands (then one strand) to make the upper stems thinner.

Dried honesty seed cases

1.   Mount the lining fabric in the hoop and trace the seed cases, seed stalks and seeds. Mark the position of the stems and seed case spikes. With one strand of 738, embroider each seed stalk with a straight stitch and the seeds with tiny satin stitch dots (six stitches).

2.   Remove the lining fabric from the hoop, cover with the organza then mount both fabrics together in the hoop, taking care to maintain accurate seed case shapes.

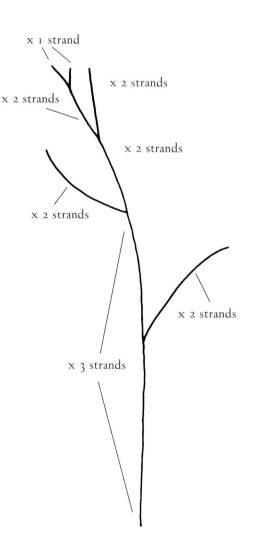

x 1 strand

x 2 strands

x 2 strands

x 2 strands

x 2 strands

x 2 strands

x 3 strands

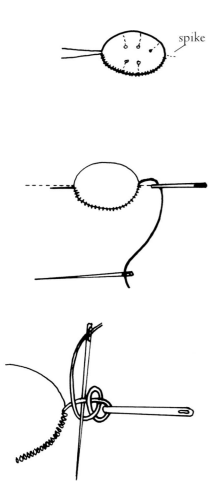

spike

Enlarged detail of spike

3.   Using tweezers, shape the uncovered wire into an oval seed case, bending each wire tail at right angles to the oval to form the stem. The wire is attached to the seed case fabric sandwich with close overcast stitches, using one strand of rayon machine thread. Starting with stitches over both the wire bends at the stem end of the seed case, overcast until halfway around the oval, opposite the position for the seed case spike. Use the same thread to work the spike.

4.   To work a detached picot for the spike, insert another needle through both fabrics at the tip of the spike mark and bring that needle out again on the opposite side of the seed case. Slide the overcasting thread under the eye end of this needle, forming a small loop. Work detached buttonhole stitches over this loop with the overcasting thread, working from the tip of the spike back to the wire edge, thus forming a small buttonholed picot for the spike. Remove the needle, releasing the picot, then continue overcasting the wire to the fabric back to the stem end of the seed case. To form the stem, wrap over both wires (not through the fabric) for about ¹/₂ cm (³/₈'') with the overcasting thread, finishing with a knot.

5.   Carefully cut out the seed cases and apply to the stems on the main fabric by inserting the wire tails through to the back of the work, using a yarn darner. Secure the wires with tiny stitches. Trim excess wire.

HEARTSEASE

This much loved wild pansy (Viola tricolor), is one of the ancestors of all modern hybrids. Also known as Love-in-Idleness and Johnny-jump-ups, Heartsease grew wild in the fields providing materials for lovers' potions and medical cures, only disappearing from pharmacists' books in 1926.

MATERIALS REQUIRED

- Calico (quilters' muslin) — 2 x (20 cm x 20 cm)

- 15 cm (6'') embroidery hoop

- Wire: Fine flower wire, cut in 12 cm (5'') lengths
  30 gauge green covered, cut in 18 cm (7'') lengths

- Purple and yellow marking pens to colour wire (optional)

- Fine tweezers to shape wire

- Needles: Crewel/embroidery 10
  Chenille 18
  Sharp yarn darner 14

- Threads: Pale yellow stranded thread — DMC 744, 745
  Medium yellow stranded threads — Madeira Silk 113
  and 114
  Dark yellow stranded thread — DMC 741
  Mauve stranded threads — Au Ver à Soie d'Alger 3322
  and 3323
  Dark purple threads — Au Ver à Soie d'Alger 1336 and 3336
  Dark purple fine silk machine thread — Silk Thread 50
  colour 24

Medium green thread — DMC 3346
Dark green thread — DMC 3345

Heartsease stems and leaves

1. Work the stems, in the order as shown on diagram, in chain stitch with two strands of 3345.

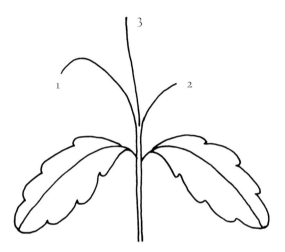

2. Embroider the leaves on the main fabric, with one strand of thread, as follows:
— central vein in chain stitch (3346)
— leaf surface in padded buttonhole stitch (3345)
— side veins with straight stitches (3346).

3. Work the detached leaves, on calico/muslin mounted in a hoop, as follows:
— couch then overcast the green wire down the central vein (3346)
— couch then buttonhole the wire around the outside edge (3345)
— embroider the leaf surface, inside the wire, in padded satin stitch (3345)
— work the veins with straight stitches (3346).

If desired, work a tiny ladybird with detached wings (see page 37) on the surface of the right hand leaf before you remove the detached leaves from the hoop. Carefully cut out the leaves.

Apply the detached leaves over the surface leaves, by inserting the wire tails through to the back of the work, using a yarn darner. Secure wires with tiny stitches then trim.

Heartsease flowers

1.   Mount the calico into the embroidery hoop and trace five petals for each heartsease. Number them from 1 to 5 as shown in diagram. The petals are embroidered with one strand of thread using the colours as indicated on the diagrams on page 33. Colour the flower wire with marking pen if desired.

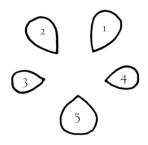

2.   Embroider the heartsease petals as follows:

(a) Starting at the base of the petal, couch the wire to the calico around the petal shape. For petals 1 to 4, leave one tail of wire with which to apply the petal. Leave two tails of wire for petal 5. Using the same thread, stitch the wire to the calico with small, close buttonhole stitches, incorporating the couching stitches and working the buttonhole ridge on the outside edge of the petal.

(b) The top third of each petal is covered by a row of long and short buttonhole stitches, worked close together and close to the inside edge of the wire. Keep the stitch direction towards the centre of the heartsease.

(c) Embroider the petal in straight stitches, keeping the stitch direction towards the centre of the heartsease.

(d) Embroider the base of the petal in straight stitches, then work purple rays with fine Silk Thread 50.

2.   Using sharp scissors, cut out the petals close to the buttonholed edge, avoiding the wire tails. The heartsease petals are attached to the main fabric by inserting the wire tails one at a time, through the same hole, using a large chenille needle. Apply the petals in the order as numbered (petal 5 is applied last), securing the wire tails with small stitches to the back of the work. It is easier to secure each petal before proceeding to the next. Trim the wires.

3.   Work the centre of each heartsease with a French knot (one soft wrap) using the chenille needle and 6 strands of dark yellow thread (741). Carefully shape the petals with eyebrow tweezers or fingers.

Purple/Yellow Heartsease

Petals 1 and 2 — 3336
— 3336
— 1336
— 1336

Petals 3 and 4 — 744
— 113
— 114
— 114

Petal 5 — 3336 and 114
— 3336 and 114
— 114
— 741

Diagrams not to scale

Mauve/Yellow Heartsease

Petals 1 and 2 — 3323
— 3323
— 3322
— 3322

Petals 3 and 4 — 745
— 744
— 744
— 744

Petal 5 — 113
— 113
— 114
— 741

Diagrams not to scale

Purple/Mauve/Yellow Heartsease

Petals 1 and 2 — 3336
— 3336
— 1336
— 1336

Petals 3 and 4 — 3323
— 3323
— 3322
— 3322

Petal 5 — 113 and 3336
— 113 and 3336
— 114
— 741

Diagrams not to scale

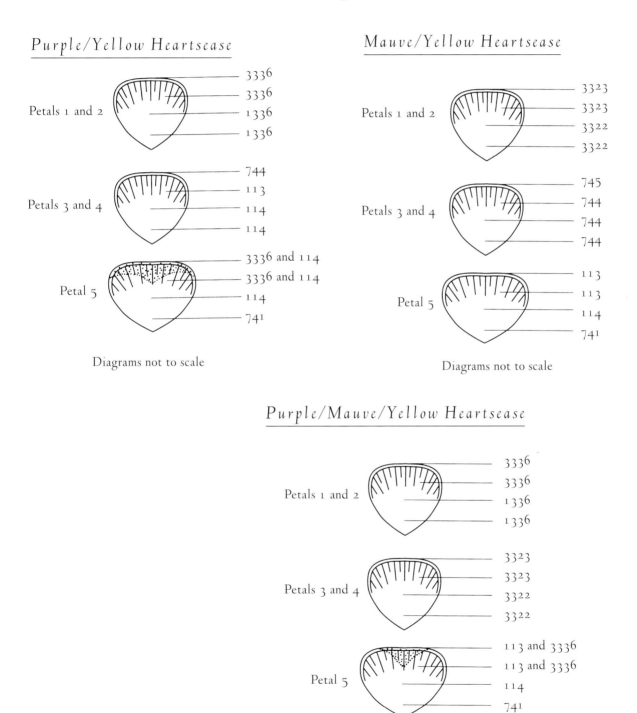

Buff-Tailed Bumble Bee

The *Bombus terristris* is very common in woods and gardens where they pollinate a great many plants, in particular cranberries, raspberries, sage, thistles and fruit trees. The queens emerge from hibernation at the beginning of spring to look for a suitable site for a nest; their search is accompanied by a deep buzzing. This species lives mostly in holes (often an abandoned mouse nest) as deep as 1 m (3 ft) in the ground, which the female bee lines with pieces of dry grass and leaves.

MATERIALS REQUIRED

- Wing fabric (cream crystal organza) — 15 cm x 15 cm (6'' x 6'')

- Cream nylon organza — 15 cm x 15 cm (6'' x 6'')

- Paper-backed fusible web — 15 cm x 15 cm (6'' x 6'')

- 10 cm (4'') embroidery hoop

- Wire: 28 gauge uncovered, cut in 12 cm (5'') lengths

- Fine tweezers to shape wire

- Eyebrow brush/comb

- Mill Hill Glass Seed Beads 374 (blue/black)

- Needles: Crewel/embroidery or sharps 10
  Straw/milliners 9
  Sharp yarn darner 14

Buff-tailed
bumble bee
wings

Threads: Dark brown/grey stranded thread — DMC 844
Copper stranded thread — DMC 921
Buff stranded thread — DMC 3033
Cream rayon machine thread — Madeira Rayon No.40 colour 1082
Gold metallic thread — Madeira Metallic No.40 colour gold 3
Bronze/black metallic thread — Kreinik Cord 215c

Thorax and abdomen

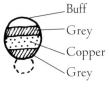
Abdomen
Thorax

1.   Trace bee thorax and abdomen on to satin and outline with small back stitches with one strand of buff thread.

2.   Work the abdomen in Turkey knots using 2 strands of thread in a straw needle. Starting at the thorax end of the abdomen, aim to stitch 2 rows of Turkey knots in grey; 3 rows in copper; 2 rows in grey and 3 rows of buff for the tail. The number of rows may vary — it depends on the size of your stitches. The Turkey knots should pierce the back stitches but not protrude outside them.

Buff
Grey
Copper
Grey

3.   Cut the loops between the knots and comb the threads upwards. Cut the threads in a curved shape, to form a velvety mound.

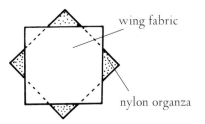

Wings

1.   Fuse the wing fabric to the nylon organza backing (one layer on the bias/cross grain if desired), using paper-backed fusible web, and mount in the hoop.

2.   Bend the wires into wing shapes, two large and two small, using the diagrams as a guide. Do not cross the wires at *.

wing fabric

nylon organza

*

3. Using one strand of rayon thread in a crewel or sharps needle, attach the wire to the fabric with small, close overcasting stitches, starting and ending at * with a few stitches over both wires. Work two large and two small wings, making sure that you have a right and a left side wing for each size. With one strand of gold thread in the straw needle, work a fly stitch in each wing for veins.

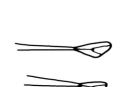

4. With sharp scissors, carefully cut around the wings.

To apply wings and finish bee

1. Using the yarn darner, insert two wings on each side of the thorax (they will be very close together within the stitched outline). Bend the wires to the sides (under the wings) and stitch to the muslin backing with tiny stitches. Trim the wing wires after the thorax has been stitched. Using two strands of thread, fill the thorax with Turkey knots, all in grey except for three knots in copper at the head end. Cut the Turkey knots to form a velvety mound.

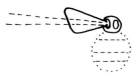

2. To form the head/eyes, stitch two beads together (from side to side) close to the thorax. Finish with one stitch between the beads towards the thorax — this makes the beads sit evenly to form the head.

3. With two strands of bronze metallic thread in the straw needle, work three back stitches for each leg. Complete by working a fly stitch for the mouth parts, with one strand of metallic thread.

TINY LADYBIRD

Ladybird, ladybird! Fly away home.
Your house is on fire.
Your children do roam.

This little rhyme has interesting origins. It started in England where the hop vines are burned after harvesting is over. These vines were usually covered with aphids and young ladybirds that were feeding on the aphids. When the hop vines were burning these small spotted beetles would take to wing and the larvae would crawl rapidly away from their homes that were now in flames.

MATERIALS REQUIRED

- Red cotton (homespun) — 20cm x 20 cm (8'' x 8'')

- 10 cm (4'') embroidery hoop

- Wire: Fine flower wire, 18 cm (7'') length

- Red marking pen to colour wire if desired

- Fine tweezers to shape wire

- Mill Hill Petite Glass Beads — 42014 (black)

- Threads: Red stranded thread (Madeira Silk 210 or DMC 349)
  Black stranded thread (Madeira Silk or DMC 310)

- Needles: Crewel/embroidery 10
  Sharps 12
  Sharp yarn darner 14

tiny ladybird

Ladybird wings

1.   Mount the red fabric into the hoop and trace the outline of the wings.

2.   With one strand of the red thread, couch, then overcast the wire to the fabric around the outline, leaving the ends of wire free at the top of the wings.

3.   Pad stitch then satin stitch the wings, inside the overcasting.

4.   With one strand of black thread, embroider a satin stitch spot on each wing.

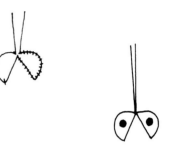

Diagrams not to scale

Ladybird body

With one strand of black thread, work the ladybird body in padded satin stitch, either on to the detached leaf surface or on to the background fabric.

To complete the ladybird

1.   Cut out the wings and apply by inserting both wires through • using a yarn darner. Bend the wires towards the tail of the ladybird and secure at the back of the leaf (or background fabric) with a few stitches. Trim the wires.

2.   With one strand of black thread, work legs and antennae in straight stitches (optional for tiny ladybird). Apply two petite black beads for eyes using the fine needle. Gently shape the wings with tweezers.

Oriental Poppy and Cornflowers

REQUIREMENTS

- Ivory satin (or fabric of choice) — 28 cm x 28 cm (11'' x 11'')

- Calico (or quilter's muslin) for backing — 28 cm x 28 cm (11'' x 11'')

- 20 cm or 23 cm (8'' or 9'') embroidery hoop

- Caterpillar (see p.51)

- Cornflowers (see p.46)

- Damselfly (see p.48)

- White Oriental Poppy (see p.41)

- Spider and Web (see p.118)

ORDER OF WORK

1. Mount the main fabric and the backing fabric into the embroidery hoop.

2. Trace the skeleton outline onto the main fabric.

3. Poppy stems and surface leaves.

4. Poppy bud and seed pod.

5. Cornflower stems and leaves.

6. Cornflowers.

7. Caterpillar.

8. Spider and web.

9. Poppy flower.

10. Damselfly.

11. Detached poppy leaves.

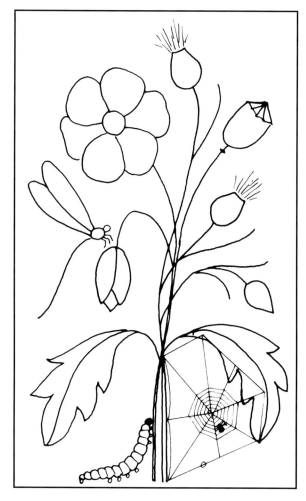

ORIENTAL POPPY AND
CORNFLOWERS

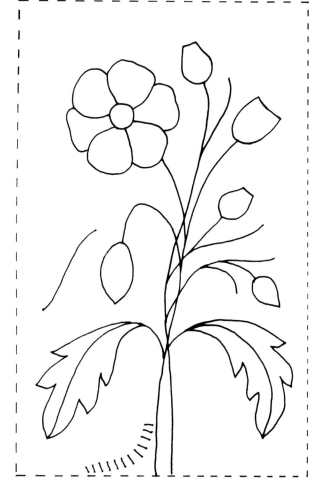

Skeleton outline

Detached poppy petal

Damselfly wings
templates

Upper wing

Poppy bud sheath

Lower wing

WHITE ORIENTAL POPPY (PERRY'S WHITE)

Showiest of the poppy genus are the many hybrids of Papaver orientale, the gigantic Oriental Poppy from Armenia. These enormous blooms shrug away their hairy sepals to unfold wrinkled crepe-like petals which may take days to reach their full diameter of up to 30 cm (12'') as a silken cup, brimming with purple-black stamens that protect the exotic seed capsule. The cultivar 'Perry's White' was developed in Britain by Amos Perry in 1913.

MATERIALS REQUIRED

- Calico (or quilter's muslin) — 3 x (20 cm x 20 cm) (8'' x 8'')

- 10 cm (4'') embroidery hoop

- Wire: Fine flower wire, cut into 12 cm (5'') lengths
  30 gauge green covered, cut in 18 cm (7'') lengths

- Fine tweezers to shape the wire

- Grey felt and paper-backed fusible web — 5 cm x 8 cm (3'' x 2'')

- White felt and paper-backed fusible web — 5 cm x 8 cm (3'' x 2'')

- Needles: Crewel/embroidery 5-10
  Straw/milliners 3-9

Tapestry 26
Chenille 18 or sharp yarn darner

- Thread: Petals — White stranded (Madeira Silk white or
DMC white)
Deep pink stranded (Au Ver à Soie d'Alger 3024 or DMC
3350)
Dark purple or black stranded (Au Ver à Soie d'Alger
3326 or DMC 310)
Centre — Dark plum stranded (Au Ver à Soie d'Alger
4636 or DMC 3802)
Green Pearl (8) thread (DMC 472)
Stems — Dark green stranded (DMC 3345)
Leaves — Mid and light green stranded (DMC 3346 and
3347)
Seed pod top — Pale green stranded (DMC 472)

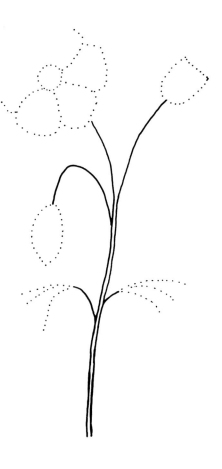

Oriental poppy stems and leaves

1.   The poppy stems are worked in stem stitch using two
strands of dark green thread (3345). Starting at the base with
two rows of stem stitch side by side (only one line is drawn
on the skeleton outline) — work one row to the flower and
one to the seed pod. Then work the stems to the poppy bud
and to the leaves as shown on the diagram.

2.   Embroider the leaves on the main fabric with one strand
of thread as follows:
— central vein in chain stitch (3347)
— leaf surface in rows of stem stitch (3346), starting at the
base and working to edge points of leaf as shown.

3.   Work the detached leaves, on calico/muslin mounted in a
hoop, as follows:
— couch then overcast the green wire down the central vein
(3347)
— couch then buttonhole the wire around the outside edge
(3346)
— work split back stitch on either side of the central vein
and inside the wire edge to provide a foundation into which
the leaf surface can be stitched.

Split back stitch

— embroider the leaf surface, inside the wire, in rows of stem stitch (3346), as for the leaf on the main fabric.

Oriental poppy flower

1.   With one strand of white thread, embroider the outside edge of the poppy petals on the main fabric in long and short buttonhole stitch (work the stitches close together, keeping the stitch direction towards the centre of the poppy). Embroider the petals in white with long and short stitches, leaving a space for the blotch at the base. Work the blotch in deep pink with a dark purple edge. Leave a small gap (1 mm) between the embroidery and the centre outline, in which to insert the detached petals.

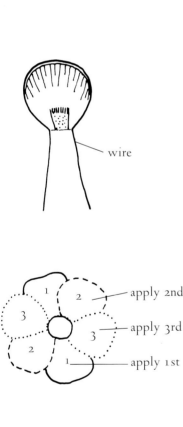

2.   To work the detached poppy petals, mount calico/muslin into a hoop and trace six petal outlines (they are easier to work if the outside edge of the petal points towards the edge of the hoop). With one strand of white thread, couch then buttonhole the flower wire around outside edge of the petal, leaving two tails of wire. Work a row of long and short buttonhole stitch inside the petal, close to the wire (work stitches close together, keeping the stitch direction towards the centre of the poppy). Embroider each petal and the blotches as for the petals on the main fabric.

3.   Carefully cut out the detached petals and apply to the main fabric, inserting the wires from each petal through two holes, using the chenille needle. As poppy petals occur in pairs, apply the petals, two at a time, opposite each other around the centre outline in the order indicated on the diagram. Bend the wire underneath each petal at the back of the work and secure with tiny stitches. Trim wire.

4.   The centre of the poppy is worked in whipped spider web stitch (p.186 🐞). Using the pearl thread (472), work four long stitches, crossing each other in the centre and extending into the petals, to form a foundation (spokes) for the whipping. Hold these threads together in the centre with a spare piece of thread. Work a whipped spider web over these foundation stitches with one strand of dark plum thread in the

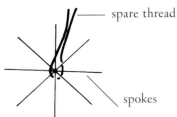

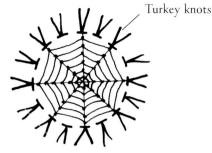

Turkey knots

tapestry needle, pulling gently on the spare thread as you whip, causing the web to be slightly raised. When whipping is complete, remove the spare thread revealing the small green centre point. With two strands of dark purple or black thread (or one of each), work sixteen Turkey knots around the whipped centre for stamen (one knot at the end of each spoke and one in between), then cut to the desired length. Shape the petals with tweezers.

Oriental poppy seed pod

1.   Using paper-backed fusible web, cut three pieces of grey felt to pad the seed pod, one the actual shape of the pod and two successively smaller. With one strand of green (3347) thread, stab stitch the smaller shapes in place, then apply and outline the larger shape with buttonhole stitch. Using the same thread, cover the pod with satin stitch, working the stitches closer together at the base to give a realistic shape.

2.   The top of the pod is worked in whipped spider web stitch. Work three stitches with the pearl thread (472) to form the five foundation spokes into the satin stitched base as shown, holding the pearl thread at point * until the whipping is complete. With one strand of pale green (472) stranded thread in a crewel needle, work the pod in whipped spider web stitch, starting at * and inserting the needle through the fabric at the beginning and end of each row. When filled, take the pearl thread to the back of the work at point * and secure. Work a French knot over point * with pale green thread if desired.

3.   To form a ridge at the base of the pod, work a bullion knot with one strand of green (3347) thread in a straw needle.

Oriental poppy bud

1.   Using paper-backed fusible web, cut three pieces of white felt to pad the bud, one the actual shape of the bud and two slightly smaller. With one strand of white thread, stab stitch the smaller shapes in place, then apply and outline the

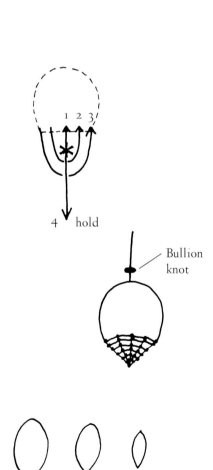

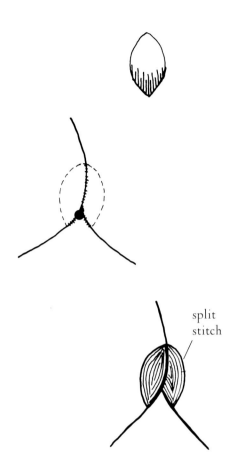

split
stitch

larger shape with buttonhole stitch. Using the same thread, embroider the lower edge of the bud with long and short buttonhole stitch, covering the outline stitches and working into the felt. Fill the lower half of the bud in long and short stitch (work the stitches softly so as not to flatten the padding).

2.   Mount calico/muslin into a hoop and trace the poppy bud sheath. With one strand of pale green (3347) thread, couch then overcast two pieces of flower wire across the lower edges of the sheath as shown, inserting one tail at ●, thus leaving three tails of wire. Using the same thread, embroider the sheath with split stitch, working in rows from the tip of the bud to the base.

3.   Cut out the bud sheath with a small seam allowance around the outside edge, and close to the wired lower edge, taking care not to cut the wire tails.

4.   Apply the sheath over the embroidered bud. Using a chenille needle, insert the top wire first, then the lower wires at either side of the bud. Secure the wires at the back, then stab stitch the outside edge of the sheath in place, turning in the seam allowance with the point of the needle as you go. Cover the stab stitched edges with a few straight stitches if required.

CORNFLOWERS

The cornflower, with its heavenly blue-purple petals, was believed to exert a magical influence over the fortunes of lovers, consequently, young men often carried it in their pockets. The botanical name, Centaurea, comes from the Greek, named after the learned centaur Chiron, who is said to have discovered the flower. The medicinal uses of cornflower were well known, the writings of Pliny recounting at least twenty remedies prepared from Centaurea.

MATERIALS REQUIRED

- Grey felt and paper-backed fusible web — 5 cm x 8 cm (3'' x 2'')

- Eyebrow brush/comb

- Needles: Crewel/embroidery 9-10

- Thread: Green stranded (DMC 3362)
  Blue/purple stranded (DMC 791, 792 and/or Madeira Silk 903)

Cornflower stems and leaves

1. The cornflower stems are embroidered in chain stitch with two strands of green thread. Work two rows of chain stitch, together or slightly apart, each row crossing the poppy stems and ending at the base of a cornflower. Then work the stem to the cornflower bud, starting at the flower stem.

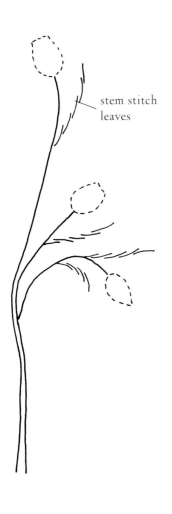

stem stitch
leaves

2.　With one strand of green thread, work the leaves in stem stitch (quite long and a little slanted).

Cornflowers

1.　Using paper-backed fusible web, cut two layers of grey felt to pad each cornflower base — one the actual size and one slightly smaller. With one strand of green thread, stab stitch the smaller layer of felt in place, then apply and outline the larger shape with buttonhole stitch.

2.　Starting at the top of the base (straight edge), cover the felt (and outline) in corded detached buttonhole stitch with one strand of green thread in a crewel needle. The laid threads (cord) are worked from left to right (using the point of the needle), and the detached buttonhole stitches are worked from left to right (using the eye of the needle), as shown in the diagram. Increase or decrease stitches at the beginning and end of rows as required. A sliver of card inserted temporarily between the stitches and the felt will facilitate the working of this covering.

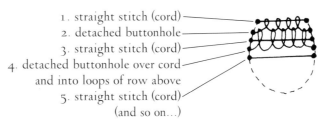

1. straight stitch (cord)
2. detached buttonhole
3. straight stitch (cord)
4. detached buttonhole over cord
　and into loops of row above
5. straight stitch (cord)
　(and so on...)

3.　Work the cornflower petals in Turkey knots (about six to eight rows), using two strands of thread, mixing the colours randomly. Cut and comb the pile to achieve the desired effect.

Cornflower bud

1. Using paper-backed fusible web, cut one layer of grey felt to pad the cornflower bud. With one strand of green thread, apply and outline the shape with buttonhole stitch.

2. Cover the felt (and outline) in corded detached buttonhole stitch as for the cornflowers, working the first laid thread (cord) a little way down from the tip of the bud. Embroider the tip of the bud with straight stitches in green or purple thread, or work a few Turkey knots.

DAMSELFLY

Small, graceful damselflies have slender bodies and narrow gauze-like wings which are held almost parallel to the body when at rest. They have large compound eyes which look like beads, and six legs which are held together to form a basket to capture insects as they fly through the air.

MATERIALS REQUIRED

- Bronze organza — 15 cm x 15 cm (6'' x 6'')

- Wing fabric (pearl metal organdie) — 15 cm x 15 cm (6'' x 6'')

- Paper-backed fusible web (Vliesofix) — 15 cm x 15 cm (6'' x 6''), and another small piece

- 10 cm (4'') embroidery hoop

- Wire: 28 gauge uncovered, cut in 12 cm (5'') lengths

- Fine tweezers to shape wire

Small piece of bronze snakeskin (or kid)

- Beads: Mill Hill Small Bugle Beads 72053 (nutmeg)
Mill Hill Petite Glass Beads 42024 (nutmeg)
Mill Hill Petite Glass Beads 40374 (dark teal)
4 mm (³⁄₁₆'') dark teal glass bead (Hot Spotz SBXL-449)

Damselfly wings
templates

Upper wing

Lower wing

- Needles: Crewel/embroidery 10
Sharps 12 (or beading needle)
Straw/milliners 9
Chenille 18 (or sharp yarn darner)

- Thread: Bronze/black metallic (Kreinik Cord 215c)
Bronze rayon machine embroidery (Madeira Rayon No.40
colour 1057)
Peacock green metallic filament (Kreinik Blending
Filament colour 085)
Nylon clear thread

Detached damselfly wings

1.   Fuse the organza to the wing fabric using the paper-
backed fusible web. Mount the wing sandwich into the
embroidery hoop, bronze side up.

2.   Bend the wires into the two wing shapes, using the template as a guide — do not cross the wires. Using one strand of
the rayon thread, overcast the wire to the fabric, starting and
ending at • with a few stitches over both wires. Work both
wings.

Upper wing

Lower wing

3.   Using the blending filament in a straw needle, work the
veins of the wing in feather stitch. Carefully cut out wings,
reserving fabric scraps for the wings on the main fabric.

Damselfly wings on main fabric

1.   Iron a piece of Vliesofix to the wrong side of the scrap of
wing sandwich. Cut out an upper and lower wing, using the
template as a guide. Fuse to the main fabric at the top of the
body line, protecting the wings and embroidery from the iron
with a piece of GLAD Bake.

2.   Work a row of split backstitch to outline the edge of the fused wings, using one strand of the rayon thread. Using the blending filament in a straw needle, work the veins of the wings in feather stitch.

To apply wings and work damselfly body

1.   Using a chenille needle, insert both the wings through one hole at A, bend the wires under the applied wings and secure to the back with small stitches. Trim the wires.

2.   The abdomen is worked with beads. With one strand of black/bronze metallic thread in a Sharps 12 (or beading needle), bring the needle up at A and thread on 4 small bugle beads (72053) and 2 petite beads (42024) and insert the needle at B (make sure the length of the stitch is longer than the combined length of the beads so that the beads sit smoothly). Bring the needle up at C, then couch between each bead back to B. Work a fly stitch for the tail and bring the tie-down thread back through all the beads to A (you may need tweezers to pull the needle through).

3.   With nylon thread in the Sharps needle, apply a small piece of bronze snakeskin over the bead-end and wires at A to form the thorax. Apply the large teal bead for the head and the small teal bead for the eye. Using the bronze/black metallic thread, work the feelers with a fly stitch and the legs with straight stitches.

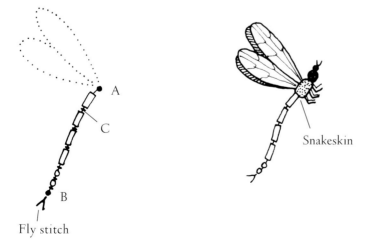

A

C

B

Fly stitch

Snakeskin

CATERPILLAR

The caterpillar (butterfly larva) has a head and thirteen segments. The head is a hardened round capsule bearing a prominent pair of toothed jaws (mandibles), a pair of short stubby antennae and six small black simple eyes on each side. The first three segments form the thorax, and each bears a pair of short, jointed legs which end in a single claw. The abdomen has ten segments, five of these bearing a pair of false legs or pro-legs. These soft, jointless structures are present on the third to sixth segments. A final pair of legs, claspers, occur on the last segment.

MATERIALS REQUIRED

- Mill Hill Antique Bead — 3036 (cognac)

- Needles: Chenille 18
  Tapestry 26
  Crewel 10
  Straw 6

- Thread: Pale lime green stranded (DMC 3819)
  Medium lime green stranded (DMC 581)
  Orange stranded (DMC 900)
  Lime green soft cotton thread (DMC Tapestry Cotton 2142)

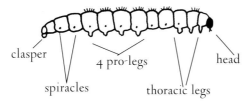

clasper

spiracles

4 pro-legs

thoracic legs

head

1.   The caterpillar body is worked in raised stem stitch. Using the chenille needle, pad the body with three lengths of the soft cotton thread. Secure the padding with 12 soft couching stitches worked in places as marked, with one strand of green thread (3819).

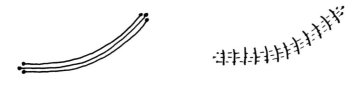

2.   Using a tapestry needle, proceed to cover the padding by working rows of stem stitch over the couching stitches. Work four rows in pale lime green, one row in orange, then about five rows in alternate greens to give a striped effect. All the rows are worked in the same direction, and enter and exit through the same two points.

3.   Work the eight legs with French knots (1 wrap) using three strands of medium lime green thread (581).

4.   Apply an antique bead for the head.

Dandelion and Buttercups

HONESTY AND HEARTSEASE

ORIENTAL POPPY AND CORNFLOWERS

OWL BROOCH OR BOWL TOP

DEER AND PEAR TREE

Wild Life

Wild beasts were a part of the embroidered gardens too. Lions with meticulously curled and waved manes sit smiling on grassy hummocks, or stand twirling their tails opposite spotted leopards, both equally disinterested in the docile unicorns, stags and camels on the surrounding slopes. The embroiderer chose these wild and mythical animals to inhabit the garden from the patterns available in books. And whether she was aware of it or not, she was following a tradition that goes back to the menageries attached to royal palaces, like the one in Oxfordshire where Henry I kept 'lyons, leopards, strange spotted beasts, porcupines, camells and such like animals.'

THOMASINA BECK, EMBROIDERED GARDENS, 1979.

DEER AND PEAR TREE

Deer and Pear Tree

REQUIREMENTS

- Ivory satin — 28 cm x 28 cm (11'' x 11'')
- Calico (or quilter's muslin) — 28 cm x 28 cm (11'' x 11'')
- 23 cm (9'') embroidery hoop
- Mound (see p.57)
- Pear tree (see p.59)
- Owl (see p.65)
- Beehive (see p.67)
- Tiny bees (see p.68)
- Spider and web (see p.61)
- Deer (see p.69)
- Pears (see p.61)

ORDER OF WORK

1. Mount the main fabric and the backing fabric into the embroidery hoop.

2. Trace the skeleton outline onto the main fabric.

3. Work the mound in rococo stitch on canvas and apply to the main fabric.

4. Tree trunk, branches and leaves on the main fabric.

5. Owl.

6. Beehive and tiny bees.

7. Spider and web.

8. Deer.

9. Detached pear tree leaves

10. Pears

11. Apply antlers.

Skeleton Outline

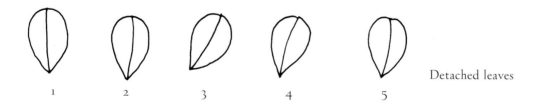

1 2 3 4 5

Detached leaves

Mound

MATERIALS REQUIRED

- Mono canvas 12 threads to 1 inch — 10 cm x 18 cm (4'' x 7'')

- Blue water-soluble marking pen

- Masking tape

- Needles: Crewel/embroidery 3-10
  Tapestry 24

- Threads: Olive green in 3 shades (DMC 731, 732, 733)

Note: Before commencing work, bind the raw edges of the canvas with masking tape. The stitching is done in the hand, not in a frame.

1.   Trace the mound outline onto the canvas with marking pen, checking that the side and lower edges of the mound line up with the threads (grain) of the canvas.

2.   Work the mound in rococo stitch with three strands of thread (one each of 731, 732 and 733) in a size 24 tapestry needle. The rows must all be worked diagonally, starting in the top right hand corner. Extend the stitches beyond the marked side and lower lines to avoid the gaps left when working rococo stitch.

3.   Place the completed mound face down on a soft towel and lightly press with a steam iron, pulling gently into shape if distorted. Leave to dry.

4.   Trim excess canvas away from all edges of the mound leaving a 7mm ($^1/_4$'') allowance. Press the top edge under, along the worked outline, keeping the side and lower edges flat.

5.   Pin the mound to the main fabric, lining up all worked edges with the skeleton outline. Using one strand of olive thread, stab stitch the top edge of the mound to the satin.

Tack/baste the side and lower edges in place (after the deer is applied, these stitches can be removed if the mound needs to be retensioned, then restitched).

6.   With the three shades of olive thread in a crewel needle, work straight stitches (imitating rococo stitch) into the top edge of the mound, to fill any gaps left in the canvas.

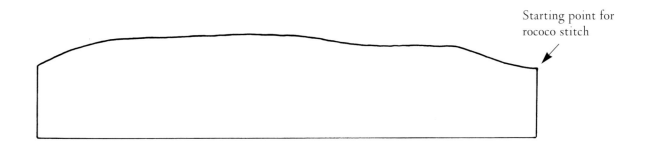

Starting point for rococo stitch

PEAR TREE

MATERIALS REQUIRED

- Calico (quilter's muslin) — 20 cm x 20 cm (8'' x 8'')

- 10 cm (4'') embroidery hoop

- Wire: 30 gauge green covered, cut in 10 cm (4'') lengths

- Fine tweezers to shape wire

- Needles: Crewel/embroidery 5-10
  Chenille 18
  Sharp yarn darner 14

- Threads: Leaves — Green stranded — DMC 469 (medium), 470 (light)
  Tree trunk — Brown stranded in 2 shades — DMC 610, 611
  — soft cotton for padding — DMC Soft (Tapestry) Cotton 2610
  Web — Silver metallic thread — Madeira Metallic No.40 silver
  Spider — Black stranded DMC 310 or Cifonda Silk — black

Tree trunk

The tree trunk is embroidered in raised stem stitch band, worked over a padding of couched, soft cotton thread.

1.   Start by couching a line of soft cotton thread around the outline of the tree (tapering to one strand at the tip of the branches), inserting this thread through to the back of the work, using a chenille needle, whenever necessary. Work the couching stitches (with one strand of brown stranded thread) as close together as needed to obtain an accurate outline.

2.   Continue to couch layers of thread on top of each other, one strand at a time, to build up the contours of the branches,

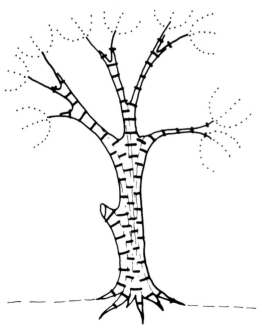

tree trunk and roots into the mound (as if working a sculp-
ture). The trunk can be as smooth or gnarled as desired.

3.   Establish a grid for the raised stem band by working
longer couching stitches over several threads, at regular intervals, along the desired contours of the trunk. These stitches
should be about 3-4 mm (⅛'') apart and not too tight. Stagger
the rows of couching stitches (and work short rows when necessary), to achieve a more realistic effect.

4.   With one strand of the darker brown thread in a tapestry needle, cover the trunk with rows of raised stem band
(using short rows when necessary for shaping), working each
row in the direction of growth, i.e. from the tree roots to the
tips of the branches. Include some rows in the lighter brown
thread for highlights. The original couching stitches can also
be used when required.

Pear tree leaves

1.   Embroider the leaves on the main fabric with one strand
of thread as follows:
— the central vein in chain stitch (470)
— work the leaf surface in padded buttonhole stitch (469)
— the veins in straight stitches (470)

2.   Work five detached leaves, on calico/muslin mounted in
a hoop, as follows:
— couch then overcast the green wire down the central vein
(470)
— couch then buttonhole the wire around the outside edge
(469)
— work split back stitch on either side of the central vein
and inside the wire edge to provide a foundation into which
the leaf surface can be stitched.
— embroider the leaf surface, inside the wire, in padded satin
stitch (469)
— work the veins with straight stitches (470)

3.   Carefully cut out the detached leaves and apply over the
surface leaves (as indicated), by inserting the wire tails

through to the back of the work, using a yarn darner. Secure the wires with tiny stitches, then trim.

Spider and web

1.   Work a fly stitch and a straight stitch in silver thread, to form the web.

2.   With one strand of black thread, work two satin stitch spots (at the end of the silver thread) for the spider's thorax and abdomen, and two small French knots for the eyes. Work eight legs, each with two straight stitches.

Pears

The pears (red Corella) are worked in needlelace over a mould of plastic modelling clay. The same technique could be used for a variety of fruits.

MATERIALS REQUIRED

· Plastic modelling material (e.g. Fimo, Polyclay, Cernit) — to match pear colour

· Needles: Tapestry 26
Straw/milliners 8

· Threads: Twisted silk thread, e.g. Kanagawa 1000 denier (colour 98)
or Kanagawa Silk Stitch 30 (colour 98)
or russet stranded cotton (DMC 355)
Brown stranded cotton (DMC 801)

Pear moulds

Knead the modelling clay until it is pliable, then break off small pieces and shape into pears. Make an assortment of shapes and sizes, some with flattened backs so that they will lie flat on the main fabric if desired. Insert a needle through the length of the pear to make a hole, then bake in an oven, on a sheet of foil, following the directions supplied with the modelling material.

FIMO — bake at 100°C-130°C (212°F-265°F) for 20-30 minutes

POLYCLAY — bake at 150°C (300°F) for 15 minutes

CERNIT — bake at 150°C (300°F) for 15-30 minutes

Select five pears of similar size, approximately 9 mm (3/8'') long — the size is your choice!

If modelling clay is unavailable, pears can be successfully made from felt, in a blending colour, rolled and stitched into shape.

To cover a pear mould with needlelace

The moulds are to be covered with a mesh of needlelace, either detached buttonhole stitch or trellis stitch, with the thread of your choice (the pears in the model are worked in trellis stitch with a fine twisted silk thread). The pears have proved to be one of the most challenging projects in classes, so the following information (gathered from these classes) is offered to enable choices to be made!

Threads: almost any thread can be used to work needlelace although some are easier to stitch with than others. The choices are:
— Twisted silk thread (1000 denier) — easiest to work, but quite coarse.
— Twisted silk thread (30 or 50 thread) — the finer the thread the more challenging it becomes! The result, however, is worth the effort.
— Stranded thread (1 or 2 strands) — is quite easy to use, and is available in variegated colours which can look very effective.

Work some samples to determine which thread you prefer. Use a fine tapestry needle and a long length of thread, as joins are to be avoided.

Work the detached buttonhole stitch (or trellis stitch), in one of the following ways (experiment and choose the method that works for you):

Method 1

(a)   Attach the pear mould to the main fabric with a long stitch through the shape and secure at the back of the work.

(b)   Take a long length of thread and tie a knot 15 cm (6'') from one end. Bring both ends up on the left side of the pear at A. Holding the short thread taut, work about 7 buttonhole stitches over it with the longer thread. Insert both threads through to the back of the work at B but do not pull tight until several rows have been stitched.

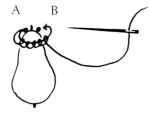

A   B

(c)   Cover the pears with buttonhole stitch, working the rows from left to right and going through to the back of the work at the end of each row. Increase at the sides of each row when necessary.

(d)   Start decreasing at the end of the pear until a circle of buttonhole stitches is formed at the base. Finish by inserting the needle through the base hole to the top of the pear, then through to the back of the work. Tighten up all the loops at the back of the work to make the mesh sit snugly around the mould.

Method 2 (worked in the hand)

(a)   Bring the thread through the pear, leaving a short tail at the base. Form a loose loop in the thread around a large straw needle (or saté stick) inserted into the top of the pear.

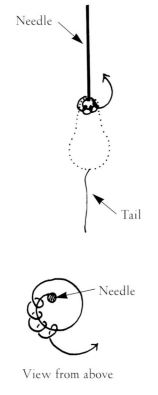

Needle

Tail

Needle

View from above

(b)   Work 8-10 buttonhole stitches around the loop (the loop will be tightened later, by pulling the tail of thread at the base).

(c)   Continue working rounds of buttonhole stitch, increasing if necessary at the back of the pear.

(d)   Decrease in the last rows at the base of the pear and, after pulling the base tail of thread to tighten the top of the pear, insert the needle from the base through to the top. Use both threads (or the top thread only) to apply the pear to the main work, at the base of a leaf.

Method 3 (worked in the hand)

(a)   Bring the thread through the pear to wrap three or four times (leaving a tail at the base), and secure by inserting a large straw needle or sate stick into the top of the pear.

(b)   Make a loop at the top of the pear, underneath the wrapped threads. Work 8-10 buttonhole stitches around this loop.

(c)   Continue working rounds of buttonhole stitch, increasing if necessary at the back of the pear.

(d)   Decrease in the last rows at the base of the pear and insert the needle from the base through to the top. Use both threads (or the top thread only) to apply the pear to the main work, at the base of a leaf.

All Methods:

Using two strands of dark brown thread, bring the needle out at the top of the pear then through to the base. Work a French knot at the base of the pear (2 wraps) then bring the needle back through to the top of the pear where the threads can be used to form a wrapped stalk, if desired.

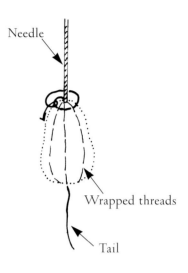

Needle

Wrapped threads

Tail

O w l

MATERIALS REQUIRED

- Calico (or quilter's muslin) — 20 cm x 20 cm (8'' x 8'')

- 10 cm (4'') embroidery hoop

- Small amount of stuffing and saté stick

- Mill Hill Petite Glass Beads 42028 (ginger)

- Needles: Crewel/embroidery 5-10
  Sharps (or beading) 12

- Threads: Beige stranded in 2 shades DMC 3032
  (medium), 3033 (light)
  Brown stranded in 3 shades DMC 3045 (light), 869
  (medium), 3787 (dark)
  Black stranded DMC 310
  Nylon clear thread

1.   Mount the calico into the hoop and trace the slightly enlarged owl head and body. The owl is embroidered using one strand of thread.

2.   Embroider the breast of the owl in long and short stitch blending the three lightest colours (3033, 3032, 3045).

3.   The wings are filled with rows of Roumanian couching worked with the two darkest shades (3787, 869). The direction of the rows can be either of the examples shown.

4. Embroider the head with straight stitches in medium shades, then work each eye with a buttonhole wheel in light beige thread (3033), and the beak with straight stitches in black.

To apply the owl to the main fabric

5.   Run a gathering thread 1mm away from the outside edge of the owl (not the base) then cut out, leaving a small turning allowance. Turn in the lower edge, then gently pull the gathering thread to ease the remaining turning allowance to the inside. Apply the owl body (below the head) to the branch with small stab stitches (make sure the owl is sitting straight on the branch!) and stuff lightly using a saté stick. Stab stitch the head in place, leaving a small gap at the top to insert the stuffing, then stitch the opening closed. Cover the stab stitches with straight stitches in blending shades, if required. Stitch along neck and wing lines with small stab stitches to sculpt the owl body.

To complete the owl

1.   The tail is embroidered in detached chain stitches of varying lengths in medium and dark shades.

2.   Each ear tuft is two detached chain stitches (one inside the other) in light and medium shades.

3.   The claws for each leg are two bullion knots, worked over the branch with black thread.

4.   Each eye is a petite bead, applied on its side with three stitches worked in nylon thread, in the middle of each buttonhole wheel. Stitch a French knot, with black thread, in the centre of each bead to complete the eyes.

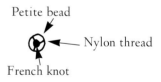

Petite bead

Nylon thread

French knot

BEEHIVE

MATERIALS REQUIRED

- Beige felt, paper-backed fusible web and organza —
  5 cm x 8 cm (2'' x 3'')

- Threads: Straw yellow stranded in 2 shades — DMC 729
  (light), 680 (medium)
  Brown stranded — DMC 3371

- Needles: Crewel/embroidery 10

1. Iron fusible web to organza (protect iron with GLAD
Bake). On organza side, trace beehive outline (and all internal
lines) and two smaller shapes for padding. Remove the paper
and fuse the organza to the felt. Cut shapes out carefully.

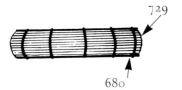

2. With one strand of the light yellow thread, stab stitch
the padding layers in place, starting with smallest layer and
keeping organza side uppermost. Stitch upper layer of beehive
in place with stab stitches at the end of each round as shown.

3. Embroider the hive entrance in satin stitch with one
strand of brown thread.

4. Using the pencil lines on the organza as a guide, embroider
each round of the beehive as follows:
— work 10 long satin stitches in 729
— work 2 long satin stitches on either side in 680
— couch all in place with 680 (keep within the pencil lines)

Repeat for each round, staggering couching stitches to form a
brick pattern.

TINY BEES

MATERIALS REQUIRED

- Black stranded thread (DMC 310)

- Yellow stranded thread (DMC 783)

- Silver/black metallic thread (Kreinik Cord 105c)

- Needles: Crewel 10

1.   With one strand of black thread, work seven small satin stitches into the same two holes to pad the body.

2.   Using one strand of thread, work satin stitches over padded body, in black and yellow (two stitches in each colour — three black stripes and two yellow).

3.   With one strand of black thread, work a French knot (2 wraps) for the head.

4.   Using metallic thread, work two detached chain stitches for the wings.

Deer

The stag, 'royal beast of the chase', has always been a popular motif, both with embroiderers and as an image in heraldry, where it signified 'a man who is wise and politicke, who well foresees his times and opportunities, endowed with exceeding speed of foot, to flie from danger when it approacheth'.

MATERIALS REQUIRED

- Calico (or quilter's muslin) — 20 cm x 20 cm (8'' x 8'')

- 10 cm (4'') embroidery hoop

- Wire: 28 gauge uncovered, cut in 15 cm (6'') lengths

- Fine tweezers to shape wire

- Mill Hill Petite Bead 42014 (black)

- Stuffing and saté stick

- Needles: Crewel/embroidery 10
  Sharps (or beading) 12
  Sharp yarn darner 14

- Threads: Cream stranded in 2 shades — DMC 739 (light), 738 (medium)
  Tan stranded in 3 shades — DMC 437 (light), 436 (medium), 435 (dark)
  Dark brown stranded — DMC 801

1. Mount the calico into the embroidery hoop and trace the deer outline and the two reference points for the mound.

2. The deer is embroidered in long and short stitch using one strand of thread (imagine that you are stroking the animal when determining the stitch/hair direction). The antlers, hooves, tail, back ear and facial features are all worked after the deer is applied to the main fabric.

A guide to the order of working and the shades used is as follows:

(a) belly and chest — medium and light cream (739, 738)

(b) spots — light cream (739)

(b) background legs — dark and medium tan (436, 435)

(c) foreground legs — dark (edges), medium and light tan (435, 436, 437)

(d) back and neck — medium cream, light and medium tan (436, 437, 738)

(e) head — light and medium cream and tan (739, 738, 436, 437).

To apply the deer to the main fabric

1. Cut out the deer, leaving a turning allowance of 5 mm (³⁄₈'') above the reference points, 3 mm (¹⁄₈'') below the reference points, and no turning allowance at the base of the unembroidered hooves. Finger press the turnings to the inside (and tack/baste if desired).

2. Pin the deer to the mound, lining up the reference points with the top edge of the mound and making sure that the deer is sitting straight.

3.   Turning in the raw edges as you go, stab stitch the lower half of the deer to the mound (1), leaving the hooves unturned and unstitched. Stitch around the internal edges of the background legs (to prevent the stuffing entering). Using a saté stick and polyester filling, lightly stuff the foreground legs of the deer.

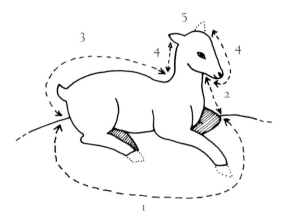

4.   Continue stab stitching the deer to the main fabric, working in the order (1-5) as shown. Stuff lightly as you go (allowing for quilting/sculpting later). Embroider the tail in light and medium cream thread.

5.   Shape (sculpt) the body of the deer with small stitches along the edges of the foreground limbs, under the head and near the tail. Hide any stab stitches that might show around the outside edge with straight stitches, worked in the direction of the hair and in blending colour/s.

To complete the deer

1.   Using one strand of dark brown thread, embroider the hooves in padded satin stitch and work the nose and mouth in straight stitches.

2.   With one strand of dark tan thread, outline the front ear with a fly stitch and work the back ear with two detached chain stitches (one inside the other). Apply a petite bead for the eye, pulling the thread firmly, then work a detached chain stitch around it.

3.   The antlers are made by wrapping uncovered wire with dark brown thread. As the antlers are fragile, do not apply to the work until all the other embroidery is complete.

Using fine tweezers, bend the wire into three branches as shown (do not curve the branches into shape until the wrapping is complete). Wrap the wire with one strand of dark brown thread (801), in the following sequence:

Tie a knot at 1, leaving a short thread tail. Wrap to 2, enclosing the tail of thread.

Take the thread to 3 and tie a knot. Wrap to 4.

Take the thread to 5, tie a knot then wrap back to 4.

Wrap the wire tails to a length longer than required for the antler, then secure the thread.

Shape the wrapped antlers and, using the yarn darner, insert the wire ends at the top of the deer's head between the ears. Secure to the back of the work and trim.

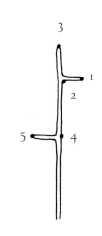

Owl Brooch or Bowl Top

This little owl makes a lovely gift when mounted into an oval brooch or pendant, or into the lid of a small porcelain box.

REQUIREMENTS

- Ivory satin — 20 cm x 20 cm (8'' x 8'')

- Calico (or quilter's muslin) — 20 cm x 20 cm (8'' x 8'')

- 10 cm (4'') embroidery hoop

- Mill Hill Petite Beads 42012 (dark pink berries)

- Owl (see p.65)

- Tiny bee (see p.68)

- Needles: Crewel 5-10
  Straw 9
  Sharps (or beading) 12

- Threads: Medium green stranded (DMC 469)
  Dark green stranded (DMC 936)
  Nylon clear thread

ORDER OF WORK

Skeleton outline

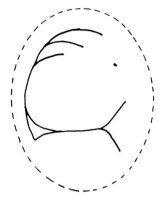

1.   Mount the satin and calico backing into the embroidery hoop. Trace the oval outline on to the calico backing, then tack/baste around this line with rayon machine thread.

2.   Trace the skeleton outline of the design on to the satin, inside the tacked oval outline.

3.   *Branch:* Embroider the branches in stem stitch with one strand of dark green thread, working two or three rows for the lower branch. Work the tree trunk in long and short stitch.

4.   *Leaves:* Embroider the leaves in fishbone stitch with one strand of medium green thread.

5.   *Owl* (see p.65). Embroider the owl then apply to the branch to complete.

6.   *Tiny bee* (see p.68).

7.   *Berries:* Using nylon thread, apply three petite beads at the end of the lower branch.

8.   To mount the embroidery into an oval frame:
— cut satin leaving a 5 mm (³/₈'') seam allowance outside the tacked outline
— cut the calico slightly smaller than the oval cardboard backing board
— gather the satin over the cardboard backing and secure
— insert into the frame and secure

Parrot and Boysenberry Bush

REQUIREMENTS

- Ivory silk or satin — 20 cm x 20 cm (8'' x 8'')

- Calico (or quilter's muslin) — 20 cm x 20 cm (8'' x 8'')

- 15 cm (6'') embroidery hoop

- Boysenberry bush and mound (see p.77)

- Parrot (see p.80)

- Detached beaded boysenberries (see p.162)

ORDER OF WORK

1. Mount the silk and the calico backing into the embroidery hoop and mark a 10 cm (4'') circle on the calico backing. Tack/baste around this circle with rayon machine thread.

2. Trace the skeleton outline of the design onto the main fabric, within the tacked circle.

3. Mound.

4. Boysenberry bush trunk and leaves on the silk.

5. Parrot.

6. Work two beaded detached boysenberries with wrapped stalks. Apply to the branch, using a chenille needle, and secure to the back of the work.

7. Detached leaves.

PARROT AND BOYSENBERRY BUSH

Skeleton outline

detached leaves

detached wing

BOYSENBERRY BUSH AND MOUND

MATERIALS REQUIRED

- Calico (or quilter's muslin) — 2 squares each
  20 cm x 20 cm (8'' x 8'')

- 10 cm (4'') embroidery hoop

- Wire: 30 gauge green covered, cut in 10 cm (4'') lengths

- Needles: Crewel/embroidery 5-10
  Straw/milliners 3
  Tapestry 26
  Chenille 18
  Sharp yarn darner 14

- Threads: Mound - fine crewel wool in shades of green —
  DMC Broder Médicis 8414, 8415, 8416 or Needle
  Necessities Over-dyed Wool colour 33
  Tree trunk — brown stranded cotton in 3 shades —
  DMC 433, 801, 898
  — soft cotton for padding — DMC Soft (Tapestry)
  Cotton 2801
  Leaves — green stranded cotton — DMC 3345 (dark),
  3346 (medium)

Mound

1. Mount a square of calico into the embroidery hoop and
trace the mound outline.

Mound outline

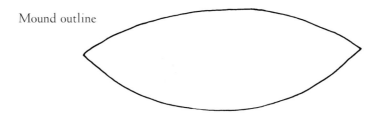

2.   With one strand of wool in the straw needle, embroider the mound in French knots (one wrap), selecting the shades randomly, unless using the variegated overdyed wool.

3.   Remove the worked mound from the embroidery hoop and trim away excess calico, leaving a turning allowance of 5mm (3/8'') around all edges. Press the turning allowance to the wrong side.

4.   Pin the mound to the main fabric, lining up the worked edges with the skeleton outline and tacked circle. Stitch the mound in place with small slip stitches using one strand of dark green cotton (3345), allowing the mound to bulge slightly.

Boysenberry bush trunk

The tree trunk is embroidered in raised stem stitch band, worked over a padding of couched, soft cotton thread.

1.   Couch a line of soft cotton thread from the mound to the base of each leaf, taking the thread ends through to the back of the work with a chenille needle. Work the couching stitch-es about 3 mm (1/8'') apart, using one strand of mid-brown thread (801).

2.   Couch several layers of soft cotton thread on top of each other, one strand at a time, to build up the contours of the trunk, taking some threads into the mound for roots.

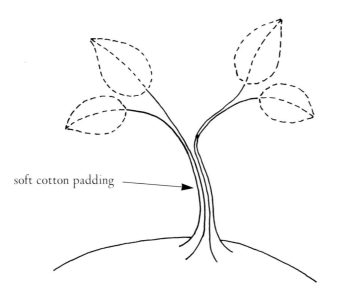

soft cotton padding

3.	Establish a grid for the raised stem band by working longer couching stitches over several threads, at regular intervals, along the trunk. These stitches should be about 3-4 mm apart and not too tight. Stagger the rows of couching stitches (and work short rows when necessary), to achieve a more realistic effect.

4.	With one strand of brown thread in a tapestry needle, cover the trunk with rows of raised stem band (using short rows when necessary for shaping), working each row in the direction of growth, i.e. from the tree roots to the tips of the branches. Work some rows in the darker brown at the edges for shading, and in the lighter brown for highlights. The original couching stitches can also be used when required.

Boysenberry bush leaves

1.	Embroider the leaves on the main fabric with one strand of thread as follows:
— central vein in chain stitch (3346)
— work the leaf surface in padded buttonhole stitch (3345)
— side veins with straight stitches (3346).

2.	Work two detached leaves, on calico/muslin mounted in a hoop, as follows:
— couch then overcast the green wire down the central vein (3346)
— couch then buttonhole the wire around the outside edge (3345)
— work split back stitch on either side of the central vein and inside the wire edge to provide a foundation into which the leaf surface can be stitched
— embroider the leaf surface, inside the wire, in padded satin stitch (3345)
— work the veins with straight stitches (3346).

3.	Carefully cut out the detached leaves and apply by inserting the wire at the base of the leaves on the main fabric, using a yarn darner. Secure the wire at the back of the work, then trim.

Parrot

This brilliantly coloured, talkative bird is part of a large family, Psittacidae, which includes cockatoos, lorikeets, macaws, love-birds and parakeets. Native to the tropics, parrots have been popular as caged pets for thousands of years.

MATERIALS REQUIRED

- Calico (or quilter's muslin) — 20 cm x 20 cm (8'' x 8'')

- 10 cm (4'') embroidery hoop

- Cream felt, paper-backed fusible web and organza —
  5 cm x 8 cm (2'' x 3'')

- Wire: Fine flower wire 10 cm (4'') length

- Teal marking pen to colour wire (optional)

- Mill Hill Petite Bead 42028 (ginger)

- Needles: Crewel/embroidery 5-10
  Straw/milliners 3-9
  Sharps 12
  Tapestry 26

- Threads: Red/orange stranded in 3 shades — DMC 900, 606, 608
  Orange/yellow stranded in 3 shades — DMC 740, 741, 742
  Bright green stranded in 2 shades — DMC 905, 906
  Teal stranded in 3 shades — DMC 3808, 3809, 3765
  Electric blue stranded — DMC 995
  Electric blue metallic — Madeira Metallic No.40 colour 37

Black stranded — DMC 310 or Cifonda Art Silk — black Nylon clear thread

1.   Iron the fusible web to the organza (protect the iron with GLAD Bake). On the organza side, trace the parrot outline (and all internal lines), and the three smaller shapes for padding. Remove the paper and fuse the organza to the felt. Cut the shapes out carefully. Cut away the shaded areas on the smaller two layers of felt to allow for the branch.

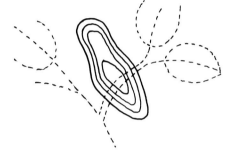

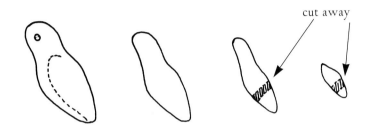

cut away

2.   With one strand of an orange thread, stab stitch the padding layers in place, starting with the smallest layer (on either side of the branch), keeping the organza side uppermost. Outline the top layer of felt with buttonhole stitch (stitches 2 mm apart), using an orange thread for the lower side of the body, and teal thread for the upper side.

3. Using one strand of thread, embroider the parrot body with straight stitches taken through to the back of the work (do not make these stitches too tight or they will flatten the padding). Work the stitches and blend the colours as follows:

(a) Starting at the tail with dull orange thread (900), work the lower half of the body (and under the wing) with straight stitches, shading from dull orange to red/orange (606 and 608), then orange to yellow (740, 741 and 742) for the lower head.

(b) Starting at the tail with dark teal thread (3808), work the upper half of the body with straight stitches, shading from dark teal to electric blue (3809, 3765 and 995), then bright greens (905, 906) for the upper head.

4. The tail feathers are worked in needleweaving over a loop of thread as follows:

(a) Using two strands of thread, bring the needle out at the tail end of the body, go down 2 mm away and secure at the back of the work, leaving a loop the length of the feather. Pass a strand of scrap thread through the loop and hold it taut with the left hand while the weaving is being done.

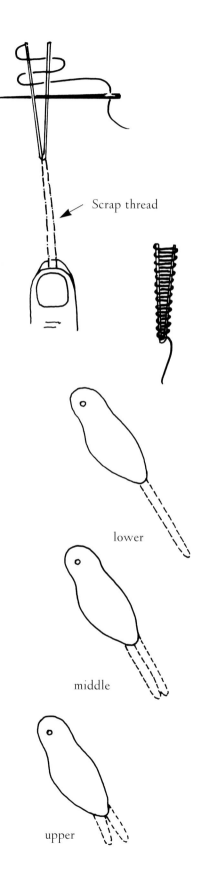

Scrap thread

(b) Using the suggested thread/s in a fine tapestry needle, fill the loop with needleweaving, taking the needle *over* the thread and *into* the loop (from right to left, then left to right and so on), so that the woven thread finishes on the *underside* of the feather end.

(c) Remove the scrap thread, then insert the tail of the woven thread (loosely) through to the back of the work at the lower end of the feather and secure to the calico backing.

Work the tail feathers in the following order, using the suggested threads.

LOWER TAIL FEATHER:
— make a loop 24 mm (1'') long with 2 strands of teal thread (3808)

— weave with 2 strands of thread: 1 dark teal (3808) and 1 blue metallic (37).

lower

MIDDLE TAIL FEATHERS:
— make both loops 17 mm (³/₄'') long with two strands of dark teal thread (3808)

— weave the upper feather with 2 strands of thread: 1 electric blue (995) and 1 blue metallic (37)

— weave the lower feather with 2 strands of thread: 1 orange (900) and 1 blue metallic (37).

middle

UPPER TAIL FEATHERS:
— make the upper loop 10 mm (¹/₂'') long with two strands of electric blue (995), and weave with one strand of the same thread.

upper

— make the lower loop 8 mm (¹/₃'') long with two strands of orange (900), and weave with one strand of the same thread.

5.   The detached wing is worked with one strand of thread as follows:

(a) Mount the calico into the embroidery hoop and trace the detached wing outline. Colour the wire with marking pen if desired. Using dark teal thread (3808), couch the wire to the calico around the wing outline, leaving two tails of wire. Do not stitch the small loop at the end of the wing.

(b) Overcast the lower edge of the wing to the calico with dark teal thread (3808). Buttonhole stitch the upper edge of the wing to the calico with electric blue thread (995). Do not stitch the small loop at the end of the wing — fill this with needleweaving using electric blue thread in a fine tapestry needle.

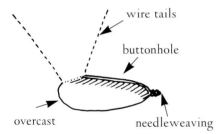

wire tails

buttonhole

overcast   needleweaving

(c) Work a row of long buttonhole stitches inside the wire, along the upper edge of the wing. Embroider the remainder of the wing with straight stitches blending in to each other (encroaching satin stitch) and into the buttonhole stitches. Use a mixture of the blue stranded threads (3808, 3809, 3765, 995) with highlights worked in the electric blue metallic thread.

(d) Carefully cut out the wing around the wire (take care not to snip the loop of needleweaving) and close to the unwired edge. Apply the wing to the parrot body by insert-ing the wires through two holes made with a yarn darner (secure to the back of the body with tiny stitches). Cover the calico wing edge (and attach the wing) with straight stitches in colours to blend with the body.

6.   Embroider the beak with straight stitches with one strand of black thread. The legs are made with bullion knots, using two strands for the leg and one strand for the claws. The eye is a petite bead applied on its side with three stitch-es worked in nylon thread. Stitch a French knot, with one strand of black thread, in the centre of the bead to complete the eye.

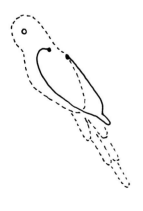

Deep Red Pansy and Beetle

Mauve Pansy/Viola and Bee

RING OF PANSIES

ORANGE RUSSET PANSY BROOCH

VIOLET PANSY BROOCH

PEA FLOWER ROUNDEL

PARROT AND BOYSENBERRY BUSH

ELIZABETHAN ROUNDEL WITH BUMBLE BEE

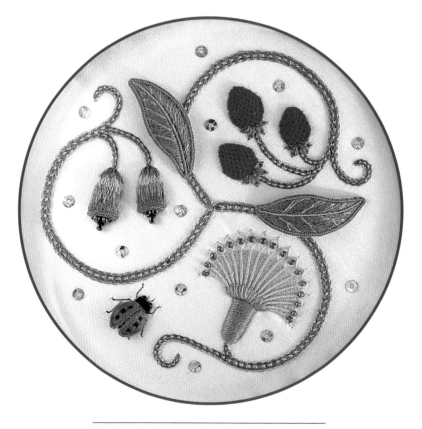

ELIZABETHAN ROUNDEL WITH LADYBIRD

Roundels

Roundel or Roundle: any circular panel that adorns a surface or an ornamental circular inset of stained glass in a window. Carved roundels were a favourite form of ornament on medieval boarded chests, and glass roundels bearing heraldic devices, set in lead-glazed windows, were known from the 15th to the 19th centuries.

DORA WARE & MAUREEN STAFFORD,
AN ILLUSTRATED DICTIONARY OF ORNAMENT, 1974.

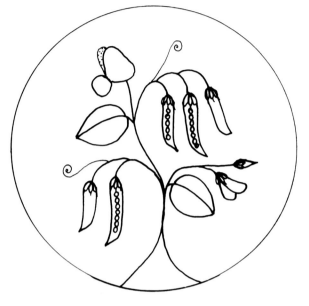

PEA FLOWER ROUNDEL

Skeleton outline

Detached leaves and petal

Pea Flower Roundel

REQUIREMENTS

- Ivory satin — 20 cm x 20 cm (8'' x 8'')

- Calico (or quilter's muslin) — 2 pieces (20 cm x 20 cm) (8'' x 8'')

- 10 cm (4'') embroidery hoop

- Wire: 30 gauge green covered, cut in 12 cm (5'') lengths
  28 gauge uncovered, cut in 12 cm (5'') lengths
  Fine flower wire 12 cm (5'')

- Mill Hill Glass Beads — 206 (violet)

- Needles: Crewel 3-10
  Chenille 18

- Threads: Green stranded thread in 5 shades — DMC 936, 469, 470, 471, 472
  Green Pearl (5) cotton thread — DMC 469
  Pink stranded thread in 3 shades — DMC 223, 224, 225

ORDER OF WORK

1. Mount the satin and a piece of muslin for backing into the embroidery hoop.

2. Trace the skeleton outline onto the main fabric.

3. Stems and mound.

4. Pea leaves on main fabric.

5. Pea flower buds.

6. Closed peapods.

7. Open peapods.

8. Pea flower.

9.   Detached leaves.

10.   Pea tendrils.

11.   A tiny bee (see p.68) can be embroidered near the pea flower if desired.

Stems and mound

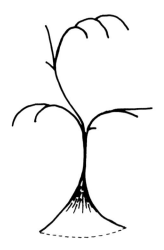

These are worked with two strands of the darker green threads (one each of 936 and 469).

1.   Starting at the base of the mound, work the stems and mound outline in stem stitch. Use one strand of either thread for the stems of the buds and leaves.

2.   Starting at the top, work the mound in long and short stitch.

Pea leaves on main fabric

These are worked with one strand of medium/light green thread (470 and 472).

1.   Work the central vein in chain stitch (472).

2.   Pad the leaf inside the outline with long stitches (470).

3.   Working from the base to the tip, embroider the leaf with long buttonhole stitches (470).

4.   Work the veins with straight stitches (472).

Pea flower buds

These are worked with one strand of thread (223, 224, 225 and 470, 471).

1.   Work the closed flower bud with straight stitches in pale pink thread (225).

2.   Embroider the sepals with detached chain stitches in light green thread (471)

3.   Work the lower edges of the open flower bud petals in long and short buttonhole stitch, then embroider in straight stitches (lower petal in medium pink 224, upper petal in pale pink 225).

4.   Embroider the sepals with detached chain stitches in green thread (470).

Closed peapods

These are worked with one strand of medium/light green thread (470 and 471).

1.   Outline the pods in backstitch (471). Pad the peapods by working three long stitches, inside backstitch outline, using six strands of thread (471).

2.   Embroider the right peapod with close buttonhole stitches, starting at the lower end of the pod, and covering the backstitch outline. Work one straight stitch at the lower end of the pod to form a point.

3.   Embroider the left peapod with two rows of close buttonhole stitches, covering the backstitch outline and each buttonhole edge being side by side down the centre of the pod. Work one or two straight stitches at the lower end of the pod to form a point.

4.   Embroider the sepals with three detached chain stitches (470).

Open peapods

These are worked with one strand of medium green thread (469 and 470).

1.   Outline the pods in backstitch (469).

2.   Apply the beads with one long stitch down the centre of each pod, then couch between each one to secure. (Make sure that there are not too many beads — allow for space to work the sepals at the top of the pod.)

3. Pad the peapod sides with two long stitches of pearl thread on each side of the beads.

4. The peapod sides are worked in buttonhole stitch (469), over the two strands of pearl thread (for padding) through to the back of the work. Use the row of beads as a support for these stitches which should be slightly raised from the surface. Start at the top of the pod and work in the direction as shown. Stitch the sides of the peapod together at the top and the bottom (if necessary) with tiny stitches, to give the illusion that the peas are bursting the pods. Work one or two straight stitches at the lower end of the pod to form a point.

5. Embroider the sepals with three detached chain stitches (470).

2 stitches of padding

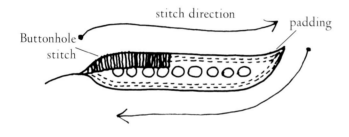

Pea flower

This is embroidered with one strand of pink thread (225, 224, 223).

1. Work the edge of the upper petal in long and short buttonhole stitch, using pale pink thread (225) and keeping the stitch direction towards the centre edge of the petal. Embroider the petal in long and short stitch in pale pink, changing to medium pink (224) at the base of the petal.

2. Using dark pink thread (223), outline the lower petal in backstitch, pad with straight stitches then embroider in satin stitches to cover the outline.

Note: The detached upper petal is worked on calico/muslin mounted in a hoop (trace the outlines and work the detached leaves at the same time).

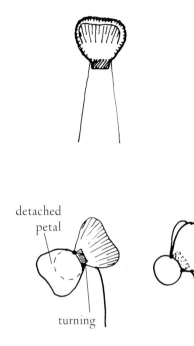

detached
petal

turning

3. Trace the upper petal shape on to calico. Couch then buttonhole the flower wire to the calico around outside edge with pale pink thread (225). Work a row of long and short buttonhole stitch inside the top edge of the wire, keeping the stitch direction towards the centre edge of the petal. Embroider the petal in long and short stitch in pale pink, changing to medium pink (224) at the base of the petal. Carefully cut out the petal, leaving a small turning (2 mm) of fabric at the lower edge (between the wires).

4. Using a chenille needle to insert the wires, apply the petal to the main fabric at the points as shown, keeping the petal face down over the lower petal. Secure the wires to the back of the upper petal. Stitch the turning to the upper petal with medium-pink thread, then curve the petal right side up to cover the turning.

Detached leaves

These are worked on calico/muslin with one strand of medium/light green thread (470 and 472).

1. Mount muslin in a hoop and trace detached leaves and pea flower upper petal (see Pea flower instructions).

2. Couch and overcast green-covered wire down central vein (472).

3. Couch and overcast (or buttonhole) the wire around the outside edge (470).

4. Work split backstitch next to the wire around all the inside edges then pad the leaf surface with long straight stitches (470).

5. Embroider the leaf in satin stitch (470).

6. Work the veins with straight stitches (472).

7. Carefully cut out the leaves and apply by inserting the wire at the base of the leaves on the main fabric, using a chenille needle. Secure the wire at the back of the work, then trim.

padding

satin stitch

Pea Tendrils

The pea tendrils are made by wrapping wire with one strand of light green thread (471 or 472). Either uncovered or green-covered wire can be used — the uncovered is finer, the green-covered is easier. (Refer p.21)

1.   Knot the thread 1 cm (³⁄₈'') from the end of the wire. Wrap over the wire (enclosing the thread tail) to the required length. Knot again, leaving a tail of thread and wire.

2.   Twist wrapped wire into a coil around a saté stick or large knitting needle to form a tendril.

3.   Using a chenille needle, insert the wire and tail of thread through to the back of the work and secure.

4.   Cut the unwrapped 1 cm (³⁄₈'') of wire close to the knot.

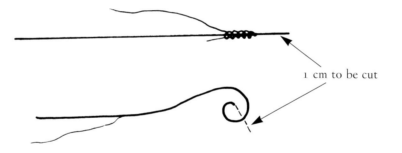

1 cm to be cut

Elizabethan Roundels

The *ELIZABETHAN ROUNDELS* were designed for a submission to the Embroiderers' Guild of America for its Seminar in San Francisco in 1996, and were inspired by the scrolling floral designs found in the embroideries of the Elizabethan period. These consisted of an all-over pattern of coiling stems enclosing flowers, birds and insects, worked in silk and metal threads, and decorated with spangles.

Garden flowers, rose, cornflower, borage, pansy, crown imperial lily, columbine, daffodil, carnation; wild flowers, thistle, convolvulus, honeysuckle, foxglove, daisy; fruit and berried plants, pear, nut, pomegranate, strawberry, grape, acorn; the peascod, transparent or open to show the peas, raindrops, birds and animals are but a few from a large repertoire freely used with the scroll.

BARBARA SNOOK, ENGLISH EMBROIDERY, 1960.

Two variations are given here, but many motifs from my first book could be used in this design.

I have very happy memories of my time spent on the west coast of the US (and Canada) in 1996.

ELIZABETHAN ROUNDEL WITH BUMBLE BEE

Skeleton outline

Detached leaves

ELIZABETHAN ROUNDEL WITH BUMBLE BEE

REQUIREMENTS

- Black or ivory satin — 20 cm x 20 cm (8'' x 8'')

- Calico (or quilter's muslin) — 2 x (20 cm x 20 cm) (8'' x 8'')

- 10 cm (4'') and 15 cm (6'') embroidery hoops

- Wire: 30 gauge green covered wire, cut in 12 cm (5'') lengths

- 3 mm (1/8'') gold sequins

- Grapes (see p. 84 🐞).

- Thistles (see p. 123 🐞).

- Acorns (see p. 36 🐞).

- Bee (see p. 44 🐞)

- Needles: Crewel/embroidery 3-10
  Straw/milliners 3-9
  Tapestry 26
  Chenille 18
  Sharp yarn darner 14

- Threads: Vine and leaves — 469, 937
  Gold thread — DMC light gold thread (Art No. 282)
  Grapes — 902
  Thistle base — 3051, 3053, 356
  Thistle top — 3607, 718, 917 (cerise)
  or 316, 3726, 3727 (dusty pink)
  or 3042, 3041, 3740 (soft mauve)
  or 340, 3746, 333 (violet)
  Acorn kernel — 3045
  Acorn base — Au Ver à Soie Perlée 455
  Bumble bee — 783, 310 (black)

White rayon machine thread (Madeira No.40 colour
1001)
Gold/black metallic thread — Kreinik Cord 205c
Sequins — Nylon clear thread

ORDER OF WORK

1.　Mount the satin and a piece of calico/muslin for backing
into the 15 cm (6'') hoop.

2.　Trace the skeleton outline onto the satin using dressmaker's carbon paper for black fabric or tracing paper (GLAD
Bake) and lead pencil for ivory fabric.

3.　*Vine.* The vine is embroidered in interlaced chain stitch:
— work the chain stitches with three strands of green thread
(937) until the branches are reached, then in two strands
— whip both sides of main vine and one side only of branches
with the gold thread (undivided) in a tapestry needle.

4.　Grape leaf, grapes and tendrils.

5.　Thistles.

6.　Acorns.

7.　Bee.

8.　*Detached leaves.* These are worked on calico/muslin mounted in a hoop, with one strand of green thread and green covered wire.

OAK LEAF:
— couch then overcast the wire down the central vein (469)
— couch then buttonhole the wire around the outside edge
(937)
— work split back stitch on either side of the central vein
and inside the wire edge to provide a foundation into which
the leaf surface can be stitched
— embroider the leaf surface inside the wire in padded satin
stitch (937)
— work the veins in straight stitches with one strand of gold
thread.

THISTLE LEAF:

— couch then overcast the wire down the central vein (469)

— couch then buttonhole the wire around outside edge (937)

— embroider the leaf surface in stem stitch filling (937)

— work the veins with straight stitches in gold (optional).

Carefully cut out the leaves and apply, using a large yarn darner or chenille needle. Secure wires to the back of the vine and trim.

9.   Apply sequins at random with nylon clear thread.

ELIZABETHAN ROUNDEL WITH LADYBIRD

Skeleton outline

Detached leaves

Foxgloves

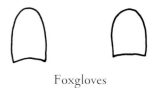

Detached ladybird wings

ELIZABETHAN ROUNDEL WITH LADYBIRD

REQUIREMENTS

- Ivory satin — 20 cm x 20 cm (8'' x 8'')

- Calico (or quilter's muslin) — 2 pieces (20 cm x 20 cm) (8'' x 8'')

- 10 cm (4'') and 15 cm (6'') embroidery hoops

- Wire: 30 gauge green covered wire, cut in 12 cm (5'') lengths

- 3 mm (1/8'') gold sequins

- Carnation (see p. 60 🐞)

- Foxgloves (see p.167 — substitute Mill Hill Antique Beads 3036)

- Strawberries (see p. 121 🐞)

- Ladybird (see p. 90 🐞 — substitute Mill Hill Petite Beads 42014 for eyes)

- Needles: Crewel/embroidery 3-10
  Straw/milliners 3-9
  Tapestry 26
  Sharps (or beading) 12
  Chenille 18
  Sharp yarn darner 14

- Threads: Vine and leaves — 469, 937
  Gold thread — DMC light gold thread (Art No.282)
  Ladybird — 900 or 666 and black
  Foxgloves — 3740, 3041, 3042, 937
  Carnation — 470, 3825 or Madeira 2307
  Green soft cotton thread (DMC Soft Cotton 2470)
  Strawberries — 321, 469
  Red twisted silk thread — Kanagawa 1000 denier —
  Colour 4 or Au Ver à Soie Perlée 779 or 664 or 107
  Sequins — Nylon clear thread

ORDER OF WORK

1.   Mount the satin and a piece of calico/muslin for backing into the 15 cm (6'') hoop.

2.   Trace the skeleton outline onto the satin.

3.   *Vine.* The vine is embroidered in interlaced chain stitch:
— work the chain stitches with three strands of green thread (937)   until the branches are reached, then in two strands
— whip both sides of main vine and one side only of branches with the gold thread (undivided) in a tapestry needle.

4.   Carnation.

5.   Foxgloves (substitute Mill Hill Antique Beads 3036).

6.   Strawberries.

7.   Ladybird (substitute Mill Hill Petite Beads 42014 for eyes).

8.   *Detached leaves.* These are worked on calico/muslin mounted in a hoop, with one strand of green thread and green covered wire.

STRAWBERRY LEAF:
— couch then overcast the wire down the central vein (469)
— couch then buttonhole the wire around the outside edge (937)
— work split backstitch on either side of the central vein and inside the wire edge to provide a foundation into which the leaf surface can be stitched
— embroider the leaf surface inside the wire in padded satin stitch (937)
— work the veins in straight stitches with one strand of gold thread.

CARNATION LEAF:
— couch then overcast the wire down the central vein (469)
— couch then buttonhole the wire around outside edge (937)
— embroider the leaf surface in stem stitch filling (937)
— work the veins with straight stitches with one strand of gold thread.

Carefully cut out the leaves and apply, using a large yarn darner or chenille needle. Secure wires to the back of the vine and trim.

9.   Apply sequins at random with nylon clear thread.

Just Pansies

Before the cultivation of what we know as pansies, wild pansies or heartsease were familiar to the Elizabethans. These tiny, fragile flowers delighted the English and Europeans who found great charm in their 'faces'. Queens and empresses grew pansies in their gardens, including Elizabeth I of England and, later, in the eighteenth century, the Empress Josephine of France, who grew heartsease in her famous garden at Malmaison.

JENNIFER ISAACS,
THE SECRET MEANING OF FLOWERS, 1993.

Pansy

Apply pansies to your choice of background fabric, either in a bunch or as part of a garland. A single pansy makes a lovely gift when mounted in a brooch or on top of a small bowl or box.

REQUIREMENTS

- Calico (or quilter's muslin) — 20 cm x 20 cm (8'' x 8'')

- 10 cm (4'') embroidery hoop

- Wire: Fine flower wire, cut in 12 cm (5'') lengths

- Marking pens to colour wire (optional)

- Fine tweezers for shaping wire

- Needles: Crewel/embroidery 10
  Chenille 18

- Threads: see requirements for individual pansies

To embroider detached pansy petals

1.   Mount the calico into the hoop and trace the pansy petals. Number them from 1 to 5 as shown. The petals are embroidered with one strand of thread using the colours as indicated on the individual pansy diagrams. Colour the flower wire with marking pen if desired.

2.   Embroider each pansy petal as follows:

(a)   Starting at the base of the petal, couch the wire to the calico around the petal shape. For petals 1 to 4, leave one tail of wire with which to apply the petal. Leave two tails of wire for petal 5. Using the same thread, stitch the wire to the calico with small, close buttonhole stitches, incorporating the couching stitches and working the buttonhole ridge on the outside edge of the petal.

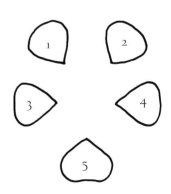

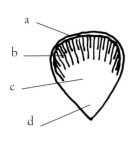

(b)   The top third of each petal is covered by a row of long and short buttonhole stitches, worked close together and close to the inside edge of the wire. Keep the stitch direction towards the centre of the pansy.

(c)   Embroider the petal in straight stitches, keeping the stitch direction towards the centre of the pansy.

(d)   Embroider blotches and/or rays at the base of the petals.

To apply the detached petals

1.   Using sharp scissors, cut out the petals close to the buttonholed edge, avoiding the wire tails.

2.   The pansy petals are attached to the main fabric by inserting the wire tails one at a time, through the same hole, using a large chenille needle. Apply the petals in the order as numbered (petal 5 is applied last), securing the wire tails with small stitches to the back of the work. For petal 5, spread and stitch the two wire tails separately to give support to the petal. It is easier to secure each petal before proceeding to the next. Trim the wires.

3.   Work the centre of the pansy with a French knot (two wraps) using a chenille needle and 6 strands of thread (keep the knot fairly loose). Carefully shape the petals with fine tweezers or fingers.

GOLD/PURPLE PANSY

THREADS

Au Ver à Soie d'Alger 3326 (dark purple), 1336 (bright purple)

Madeira Stranded Silk 113, 114 (two shades of bright yellow)

DMC Stranded Cotton 740 (orange), 741 (orange/yellow)

1.   Follow the general instructions to work the detached pansy petals, using the colours as indicated on the diagram.

2.   Apply the detached petals to the main fabric.

3.   Work the centre with 6 strands of thread (3 each of 740 and 741).

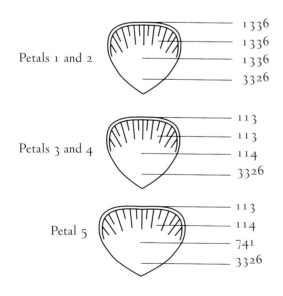

Petals 1 and 2
— 1336
— 1336
— 1336
— 3326

Petals 3 and 4
— 113
— 113
— 114
— 3326

Petal 5
— 113
— 114
— 741
— 3326

Diagrams not to scale

GOLD/YELLOW PANSY

THREADS

Au Ver à Soie d'Alger 4636 (very dark plum)

Au Ver à Soie d'Alger 611, 612 (two shades of orange/yellow)

DMC Stranded Cotton 3830 (terracotta), 742 (dark yellow)

Cifonda Silk 174 (orange/yellow)

1.   Follow the general instructions to work the detached pansy petals, using the colours as indicated on the diagram.

2.   Apply the detached petals to the main fabric.

3.   Work the centre with 6 strands of thread (3 each of 742 and 174).

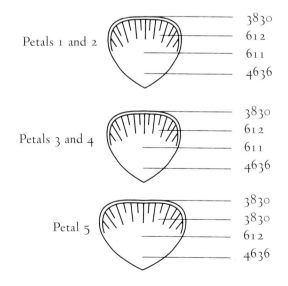

Petals 1 and 2 — 3830 / 612 / 611 / 4636

Petals 3 and 4 — 3830 / 612 / 611 / 4636

Petal 5 — 3830 / 3830 / 612 / 4636

Diagrams not to scale

Mauve Pansy/Viola

THREADS

Au Ver à Soie d'Alger 1316 (bright purple/mauve)

DMC Stranded Cotton 550 (dark violet), 742 (dark yellow)

Minnamurra Stranded Cotton 110 (variegated mauve/yellow)

Cifonda Silk 174 (orange/yellow)

1. Follow the general instructions to work the detached pansy petals, using the colours as indicated on the diagram.

2. Apply the detached petals to the main fabric.

3. Work the centre with 6 strands of thread (3 each of 742 and 174).

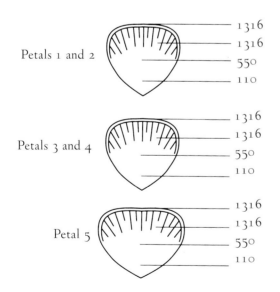

Petals 1 and 2
— 1316
— 1316
— 550
— 110

Petals 3 and 4
— 1316
— 1316
— 550
— 110

Petal 5
— 1316
— 1316
— 550
— 110

Diagrams not to scale

ORANGE RUSSET PANSY

THREADS

Au Ver à Soie d'Alger 3326 (dark purple), 616 (rust)

Au Ver à Soie d'Alger 645, 646 (two shades of orange)

DMC Stranded Cotton 742 (dark yellow)

Cifonda Silk 174 (orange/yellow)

1. Follow the general instructions to work the detached pansy petals, using the colours as indicated on the diagram.

2. Apply the detached petals to the main fabric.

3. Work the centre with 6 strands of thread (3 each of 742 and 174).

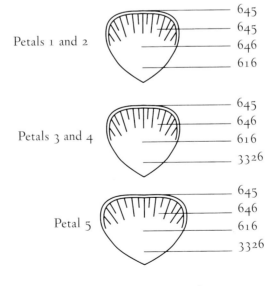

Petals 1 and 2
— 645
— 645
— 646
— 616

Petals 3 and 4
— 645
— 646
— 616
— 3326

Petal 5
— 645
— 646
— 616
— 3326

Diagrams not to scale

Deep Red Pansy

THREADS

Au Ver à Soie d'Alger 2926 (very dark red)

Au Ver à Soie d'Alger 4636 (very dark plum)

DMC Stranded Cotton 3830 (terracotta), 742 (dark yellow)

Minnamurra Stranded Cotton 110 (variegated mauve/yellow)

Cifonda Silk 174 (orange/yellow)

1. Follow the general instructions to work the detached pansy petals, using the colours as indicated on the diagram.

2. Apply the detached petals to the main fabric.

3. Work the centre with 6 strands of thread (3 each of 742 and 174).

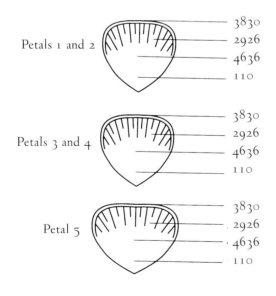

Petals 1 and 2
— 3830
— 2926
— 4636
— 110

Petals 3 and 4
— 3830
— 2926
— 4636
— 110

Petal 5
— 3830
— 2926
— 4636
— 110

Diagrams not to scale

ROYAL PURPLE PANSY

THREADS

Au Ver à Soie d'Alger 1336 (bright purple)

DMC Stranded Cotton 939 (dark navy blue), 742 (dark yellow)

Cifonda Silk 125 (purple), black, 174 (orange/yellow)

1.   Follow the general instructions to work the detached pansy petals, using the colours as indicated on the diagram. Embroider rays in black silk at the base of the petals.

2.   Apply the detached petals to the main fabric.

3.   Work the centre with 6 strands of thread (3 each of 742 and 174).

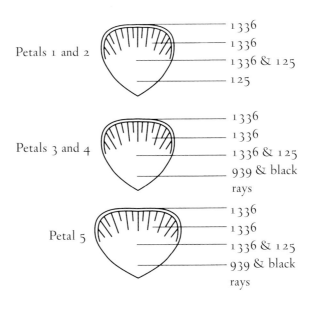

Petals 1 and 2 — 1336 / 1336 / 1336 & 125 / 125

Petals 3 and 4 — 1336 / 1336 / 1336 & 125 / 939 & black rays

Petal 5 — 1336 / 1336 / 1336 & 125 / 939 & black rays

Diagrams not to scale

VIOLET/PURPLE PANSY

THREADS

Au Ver à Soie d'Alger 3326 (dark purple)

Au Ver à Soie d'Alger 1343, 1344, 1345 (three shades of violet)

DMC Stranded Cotton 741 (orange/yellow)

Cifonda Silk 174 (orange/yellow)

1.   Follow the general instructions to work the detached pansy petals, using the colours as indicated on the diagram.

2.   Apply the detached petals to the main fabric.

3.   Work the centre with 6 strands of thread (3 each of 741 and 174).

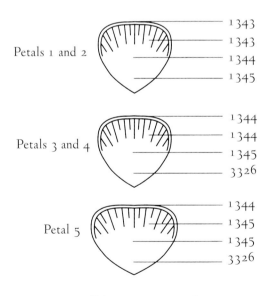

Petals 1 and 2
- 1343
- 1343
- 1344
- 1345

Petals 3 and 4
- 1344
- 1344
- 1345
- 3326

Petal 5
- 1344
- 1345
- 1345
- 3326

Diagrams not to scale

Single Pansy Brooch

Detached pansy petals are applied over embroidered leaves, then mounted into a purchased brooch form, bowl or box.

REQUIREMENTS

- Ivory satin (or fabric of choice) — 20 cm x 20 cm (8'' x 8'')

- Calico (or quilters' muslin) — 20 cm x 20 cm (8'' x 8'')

- 10 cm (4'') embroidery hoop

- Detached pansy petals of choice

- Needles: Crewel/embroidery 10
  Chenille 18

- Threads: Green stranded thread for leaves (DMC 3345)

ORDER OF WORK

1.   Mount the main fabric and calico/muslin backing into the embroidery hoop.

2.   Trace the outline of leaves onto the main fabric.

3.   The leaves are embroidered with one strand of green thread as follows:
— Work the central vein in chain stitch.
— Pad the leaf surface with straight stitches.
— Embroider each side of the leaf in buttonhole stitch, inserting the needle close to the central vein, with the button-holed edge forming the edge of the leaf. Work the stitches from the base of the leaf to the point, at an angle, and very close together.

4.   Following the instructions for single pansies (see p.104), apply the petals over the leaves, then work the pansy centre.

5.   This project can be mounted into a Framecraft brooch,

rosewood bowl or porcelain box, with the following alter-
ations to the assembly procedure:
— trim the calico backing to a circle slightly smaller than the
cardboard template/backing plate supplied
— with a small seam allowance, gather the main fabric only
over the cardboard, the calico backing becoming an additional
padding layer
— insert the pansy into the empty frame — the acetate supplied will not be used.

Ring of Pansies

This garland of pansies (Gold/yellow pansy,
Gold/purple pansy and Royal purple pansy) looks pretty
mounted into a gilt pincushion. Substitute your own colours
or use any combination of the seven pansies provided.

Skeleton outline

REQUIREMENTS

- Ivory satin —20 cm x 20 cm (8'' x 8'')

- Calico (or quilter's muslin) — 2 pieces, 20 cm x 20 cm (8'' x 8'')

- 10 cm (4'') embroidery hoop

- Wire: 28 gauge uncovered or fine flower wire, cut in 12 cm (5'') lengths

- Marking pens to colour the wire if desired

- Needles: Crewel/embroidery 5-10
  Straw/milliners 1 or 3
  Chenille 18

- Threads: Stems and leaves — dark and medium green stranded (DMC 3345, 3346)
  Pansies — see individual directions for threads and colours

ORDER OF WORK

1. Mount the satin and one piece of calico/muslin for backing into a 10 cm (4'') embroidery hoop.

2. Trace the skeleton outline onto the satin.

3. *Stems.* Work the stems in whipped chain stitch with dark green thread (3345). Use three strands for the central ring and two strands for the pansy bud stems.

4. *Leaves.* The leaves are embroidered with one strand of thread:
— work the central vein in chain stitch (3346)
— pad the leaf surface with straight stitches (3345)
— embroider each side of the leaf in buttonhole stitch, inserting the needle close to the central vein, with the buttonholed edge forming the edge of the leaf. Work the stitches from the base of the leaf to the point, at an angle and very close together (3345)
— the veins are worked with straight stitches (3346), if desired.

5.   *Pansy Buds.* The buds are worked with one strand of thread in colours to match each pansy:
— work the lower edge in long and short buttonhole stitch, then embroider the bud with straight stitches in desired colour/s
— using two strands of green thread, work three detached chain stitches at the base of each bud to form the sepals.

6. *Pansy Petals.* Mount the remaining piece of calico into a hoop and trace pansy petals (5 petals for each pansy):
— follow individual instructions to work the five detached petals for each of the three pansies
— using small, sharp scissors, cut out the petals close to the buttonholed edge, avoiding the wire tails
— the pansy petals are attached to the main fabric by inserting the wire tails, one at a time, through the same hole, using a large chenille needle. Apply the petals in the order as numbered (petal 5 is applied last), securing the wire tails to the calico backing with small stitches. Secure each petal before proceeding to the next. Trim the wires
— work the centre of each pansy with a French knot (two soft wraps) using a chenille (or straw) needle and 6 strands of thread (3 each of both yellows)
— carefully shape petals with eyebrow tweezers or fingers.

Finishing

The finished piece can be mounted into the lid of a Framecraft Gilded Pincushion 8 cm (3'') following the enclosed directions.

Another option is to convert the pincushion into a frame, using only the gilded metal base and rim:
— cut out embroidery with a 2 cm (1'') seam allowance and gather over a circle of cardboard the same size as the pincushion
— insert into the base of the pincushion, securing with a little glue if desired
— glue a circle of perspex or glass inside the rim and secure to the base
— a small brass ring can be glued to the back of the base to enable the frame to be hung.

Pansy and Beetle

This design can be worked with any coloured pansy, and a bee instead of a beetle if desired. When mounted in a small paperweight it makes a lovely gift.

REQUIREMENTS

- Ivory satin — 20 cm x 20 cm (8'' x 8'')

- Calico (or quilter's muslin) — 2 pieces (20 cm x 20 cm) (8'' x 8")

- 10 cm (4'') embroidery hoop

- Wire: 30 gauge green-covered, 12 cm (5'') length

- Pansy (see p.104)

- Beetle (see p.120)

- Small snail (see p.116)

- Needles: Crewel/embroidery 5-10
  Straw/milliners 3-9
  Chenille 18
  Sharp yarn darner 14

- Threads: Stems and leaves — three shades of green (DMC 3346, 3345, 895)
  Beetle — blue/grey (DMC 930 or Cifonda Silk 215)
  Pansy — choice of colour — see individual pansy directions for threads
  Snail — own choice of stranded threads for body and shell

Skeleton outline

ORDER OF WORK

1. Mount the satin and a piece of calico/muslin for backing into the hoop.

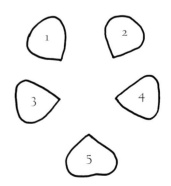

Detached pansy petals

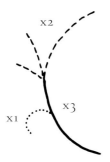

Detached pansy leaf

2. Trace the skeleton outline onto the satin.

3. *Stems.* Embroider the stems with whipped chain stitch in dark green thread (895). Work the chain stitches and the whipping with the number of threads indicated on the diagram.

4. *Leaf on main fabric.* This leaf is worked with one strand of green thread:
— work the central vein in chain stitch (3346)
— pad the leaf surface inside the outline with long stitches (3345)
— working from the base to the tip, embroider the leaf with long buttonhole stitches (3345)
— work the veins in straight stitches (3346).

5. *Pansy bud.* The bud is worked with one strand of thread in colours to match the pansy.
— work the lower edge in long and short buttonhole stitch, then embroider the bud in straight stitches
— using two strands of green thread (3345), work three detached chain stitches at the base of the bud to form the sepals.

6. Small Snail.

7. Beetle.

8. Pansy.

9. *Detached leaf.* This is worked on calico mounted in a hoop with one strand of green thread and green-covered wire:
— couch then overcast the wire down the central vein (3346)
— couch then buttonhole the wire around outside edge (3345)
— pad stitch leaf and work split backstitch around inside edge of wire (3345)
— work leaf in satin stitch (3345)
— work veins in straight stitches (3346).

10. Assemble into paperweight if desired.

BEETLE

Never kill a beetle, but leave him to go about his important work in the garden. If a black beetle crawls over your shoe, it is a warning against illness which bids you to take better care of your health. Many nocturnal flying beetles predict fine weather.

CLAIRE NAHMAD, GARDEN SPELLS, 1994.

MATERIALS REQUIRED

- Pad for working detached buttonhole stitch (see p 17)

- Wire: 28 gauge uncovered, 15 cm (6'') length
  (or 30 gauge blue-covered wire is easier to manage)

- Fine tweezers to shape wire

- Grey felt and paper-backed fusible web — 5 cm x 8 cm
  (3'' x 2'')

- Blue/bronze snakeskin — small piece

- Mill Hill Petite Glass Beads — 40374 (blue/black)

- Needles: Crewel 3-9
  Tapestry 26
  Chenille 18
  Sharps needles 12

- Thread: Blue/grey stranded (DMC 930 or Cifonda Silk
  215)
  Slate blue metallic thread (Kreinik Cord 225c)
  Nylon clear thread

Detached wings (elytra)

1.   Wrap the middle 5 cms (2'') approximately of the wire with one strand of the blue/grey thread, leaving a tail at each end.

2.   Transfer the wing outline to the buttonhole pad and cover with self-adhesive plastic (see p. 17). Tack the wrapped wire around the wing outline, leaving two tails of wire (mostly not wrapped) as shown.

3.   With one strand of metallic thread in the tapestry needle, work a row of buttonhole stitch over the wire around the inside of one wing, then work about three rows of corded detached buttonhole stitch to fill the wing. Repeat for the other wing. Remove the tacking stitches to release the wings.

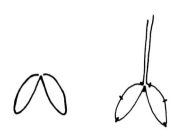

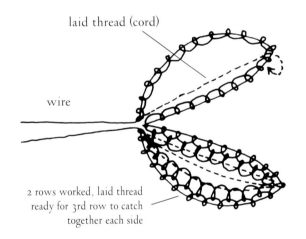

laid thread (cord)

wire

2 rows worked, laid thread ready for 3rd row to catch together each side

Abdomen

1. Using the paper-backed fusible web, cut two pieces of grey felt to pad the abdomen; one the actual shape of the abdomen and one sightly smaller.

2. With one strand of the blue/grey thread, stab stitch the felt in place (applying the smaller shape first), then cover the felt with satin stitch, worked from side to side to represent the segments of the abdomen.

To apply detached wings and complete beetle

1.   Insert the wires and any thread tails at • using a chenille needle (or large yarn darner), bend under the abdomen and secure at the back with a few small stitches.

2.   With blue/grey thread, work a few satin stitches at • for padding under the head. The head is cut from snakeskin and applied with nylon thread in a sharps needle. Cut the snakeskin a little larger than the head shape, then trim to size as you apply — make sure it is wide enough to cover the top of the wings.

Attach the snakeskin head at five points as follows:
—   work the first two stitches on either side of the wings (1 and 2)
—   make one stitch at centre front (3)
—   on either side of the centre apply two petite beads for the eyes with 2-3 stitches into the snakeskin (4 and 5).

3.   With two strands of the metallic thread in a straw needle, work three backstitches for each leg. Complete by working a fly stitch for the feelers with one strand of metallic thread.

eye — 3 stitches

Needlework Accessories and Gifts

Needlework Accessories

This group of needlework accessories consists of a small silk pouch containing a pin wheel, thimble pipkin, scissors scabbard and needlebook all embellished with raised embroidery and beads.

GENERAL REQUIREMENTS

- Bronze silk (or fabric of choice) — 50 cm x 115 cm (20" x 45")

- Good quality calico (or quilter's muslin) — 50 cm x 115 cm (20" x 45")

- Pellon (thin wadding) — 50 cm (½ yard)

- 10 cm (4") and 20 cm (8") embroidery hoops

- Thin cardboard — 1 mm (¹⁄₁₆") or template plastic

- Tracing paper (GLAD Bake)

- Paper-backed fusible web (e.g. Vliesofix) — 50 cm (½ yard)

- Paper glue (e.g. UHU glue stick)

- Craft knife and cutting board (or scissors)

- Emery board (or fine sandpaper)

- Fine HB lead pencil

- Fine ball-point pen (can be empty) for tracing

- Ruler and set square

- Silk pouch (see p.147)

- Needlebook (see p.142)

- Pin wheel (see p.131)

- Scissors scabbard (see p.138)

- Thimble pipkin (see p.134)

- Needles: Crewel/embroidery 3-10
  Straw/milliners 3-9
  Tapestry 26
  Sharps (or beading) 12
  Chenille 18

- Threads: Fine machine thread (in a contrasting colour) for tacking/basting (preferably Silk 50 or Rayon 40)
  Bronze (or colour to match silk) machine thread
  Bronze (or colour to match silk) stranded thread to join the cardboard shapes (DMC 610, 611)

GENERAL PREPARATION

Silk

Cut the silk into pieces as indicated on the diagram. If the fabric is 112 cm (44″) wide, reduce the width of all pieces except the pouch. If the fabric is less than 112 cm (44″) wide you will need an extra 25 cm (10″).

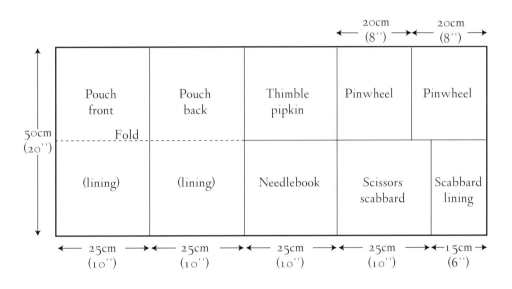

Calico/Muslin

Cut the calico into pieces as indicated on the diagram. It is used as a backing and for the embroidered applied elements (owl and foxgloves).

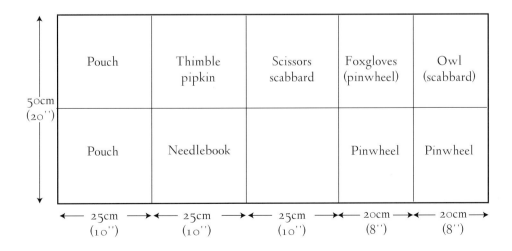

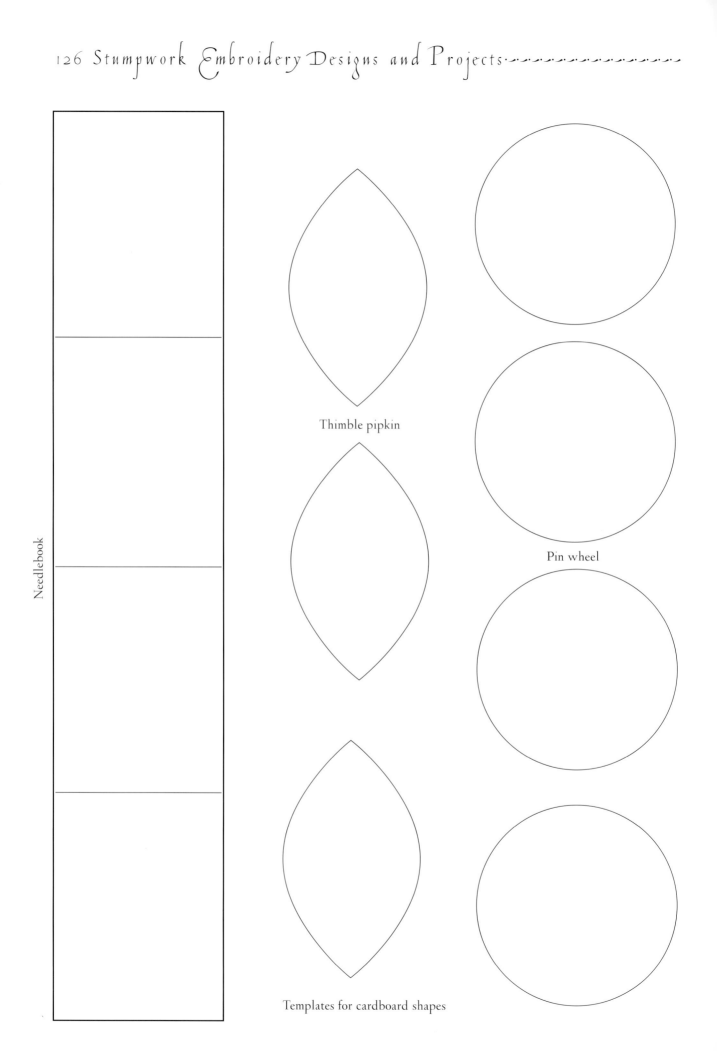

Needlebook

Thimble pipkin

Pin wheel

Templates for cardboard shapes

Cardboard Shapes

(Template plastic may be substituted for cardboard.)

1. Trace or photocopy template outlines onto paper then glue to cardboard.

Note: When working with glue and cardboard, dry the shapes under heavy books to prevent buckling.

2. Cut out the shapes with a craft knife or scissors. Glue two circles together (see *Note*) for each pin wheel shape, and two rectangles together for each needlecase shape, as a thicker cardboard is better for these items. Smooth the edges of all pieces with an emery board. You should now have the following cardboard shapes:

Pin wheel	— 2 circles
Thimble pipkin	— 3 segments
Needlebook	— 2 rectangles
Scissors scabbard	— 1 front and 1 back
	— 1 front lining and 1 back lining

3. Attach a layer of pellon to one side of each cardboard shape using paper-backed fusible web and an iron (or glue). When using the fusible web, use a pressing cloth and minimum pressure with the iron so as not to flatten the pellon too much.

4. Iron a piece of paper-backed fusible web to the other side of each cardboard shape except those required for the needlecase. Do not remove the paper until assembling the article. (Step 4 is optional).

fusible web

pellon

cardboard

Templates for cardboard shapes

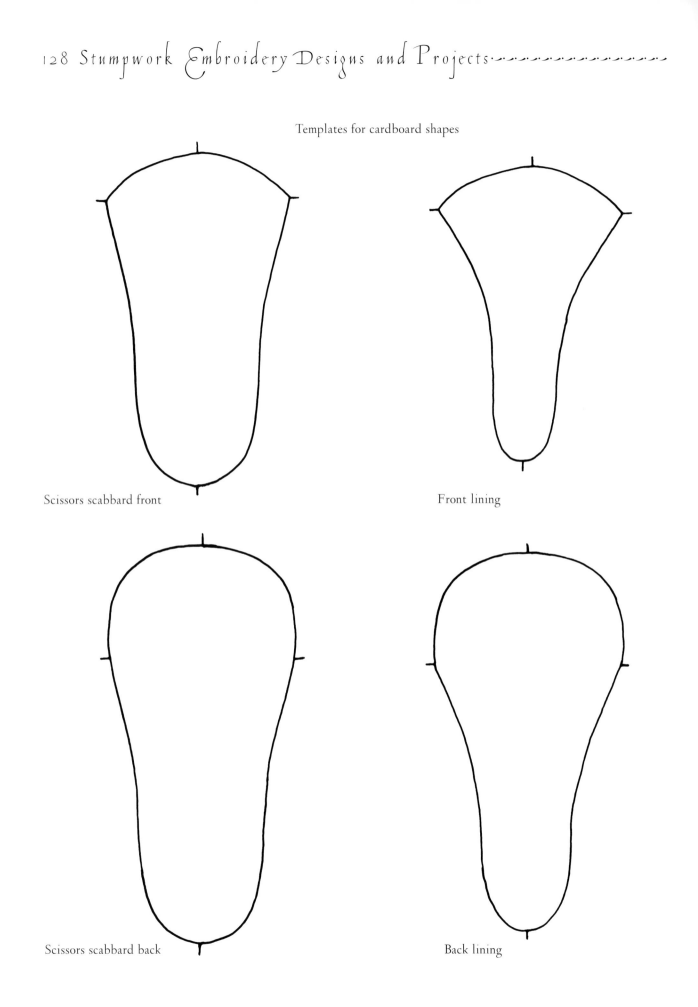

Scissors scabbard front

Front lining

Scissors scabbard back

Back lining

GENERAL INSTRUCTIONS

TRANSFERRING A DESIGN TO THE BACK OF MAIN FABRIC

Note: The following method is useful when it is preferable to have the design on the back of the main fabric e.g. when the fabric is coloured or patterned.

To ensure that your design is the right way up on the main fabric, transfer the *skeleton outline* to the calico backing fabric as follows:

1. Transfer the template shape onto the calico backing with marking pen or pencil. Tack/baste around this shape with rayon machine thread.

2. Trace the template shape and the skeleton outline of the design on to tracing paper (I use GLAD Bake) with lead pencil.

3. Place the tracing *right (pencil) side down* on to the calico backing, within the tacked template shape.

4. Draw over the skeleton outline with an empty ballpoint pen (or pencil), thus transferring the pencil outline onto the calico backing.

TO EMBROIDER FROM A DESIGN ON THE BACK OF THE MAIN FABRIC

Embroider the design on the main fabric using one of the following methods:

1. *Thread trace* the design through to the main fabric by working a row of small running stitches along the skeleton outline with silk or rayon machine thread. Remove the tracing threads as you embroider.

2. Another option is to outline the design on the main fabric in backstitch, using the traced outline on the calico backing as a guide. The backstitches will be covered by embroidery.

3.   You can also embroider the design without a thread tracing or backstitches, by referring to the back of the work as you stitch.

JOINING CARDBOARD SHAPES

You will need:

— Fabric covered cardboard shapes

— Bronze stranded thread (two strands of 611 and one strand of 610)

— Straw/milliners needle size 7

With the wrong sides facing, join both edges of cardboard together with Palestrina knot stitch, working the stitches quite firmly and fairly close together. It is a good idea to work a sample first to ascertain the tension required.

Pin wheel

Foxgloves, worked separately then applied within a wreath of leaves decorate one side of the pin wheel; a dragonfly with metallic wings and beaded body, the other. The circles are joined together with Palestrina knot stitch. Pins can then be inserted around the outside edge.

REQUIREMENTS

- Bronze silk — 2 squares 20 cm x 20 cm (8'' x 8'')

- Calico/muslin — 2 squares 20 cm x 20 cm (8'' x 8'')

- 10 cm (4'') embroidery hoop

- Prepared cardboard shapes (see p.127)

- Cream woollen doctor flannel or felt — 4 cm (1⅝'') circle

- Dragonfly (see p.165)

- Foxgloves (see p.167)

- Threads: Dark green stranded (DMC 937 or Au Ver à Soie d'Alger 2126)
  Bronze stranded (DMC 610, 611)

Skeleton outline

ORDER OF WORK

1. Mount a square of silk and a calico backing into a 10 cm (4'') hoop. Using the cardboard shape as a template, mark the pin wheel outline on the calico backing. Tack/baste around the outline with rayon machine thread.

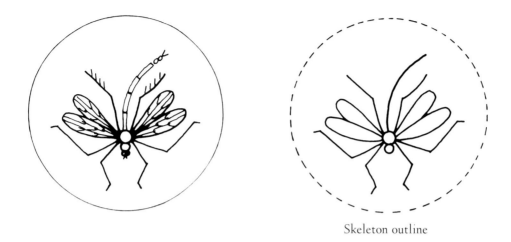

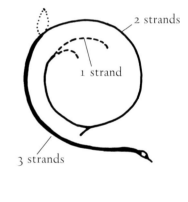

Skeleton outline

2.   Trace the skeleton outline of the design onto the calico backing, inside the tacked circle (see p.129).

Repeat Steps 1 and 2 for the other side of the pin wheel.

3.   *Foxglove stems and leaves*
Thread trace the stems from the skeleton outline, then embroider in whipped chain stitch with dark green thread (937 or 2126), removing the tracing threads as you work. Starting at the base of the stem, work the chain stitch with three strands of thread to the first single leaf, two strands to the flower stems then 1 strand to the foxgloves. Whip all stems with one strand of thread, finishing the base with a detached chain stitch.

2 strands

1 strand

3 strands

Using one strand of dark green thread, outline each leaf in backstitch, using the traced outline on the calico backing as a guide, then embroider in padded satin stitch.

4.   Foxgloves (see p.167).

5.   Dragonfly (see p.165)

TO COMPLETE THE PIN WHEEL

You will need:

— two prepared cardboard circles

— strong thread for gathering

— iron and pressing cloth (and/or GLAD Bake)

— circle of woollen flannel or felt

— bronze thread in a size 7 straw needle (two strands of 611 and one strand of 610).

1.   Remove the paper backing (from the fusible web) from the other side of the prepared cardboard circles (see Step 4, p.127).

2.   Cut out the embroidered pin wheel shape, leaving a 2 cm (1'') turning allowance outside the tacked/basted outline on both the silk and the calico backing. Run a row of gathering stitches within this allowance, using strong thread.

3.   Gather the embroidery around one cardboard shape (pellon side against the calico backing), having the cardboard aligned with the tacked outline. Secure the gathering thread and work a few lacing stitches. Remove the tacking/basting. Press the gathered turning allowance to flatten (and fuse to the cardboard if using fusible web).

4.   Repeat for the other side of the pin wheel. Insert the circle of flannel (or felt) between the two shapes (to protect the pins).

5.   Join the cardboard circles together with Palestrina knot stitch. Pins can then be inserted around outside edge, between the knots.

Thimble Pipkin

The three segments which make up the pipkin are embroidered with a padded hedgehog with silken spines; a spider web and spider (for luck); and a tiny vine enclosing your initials (for the base). The shapes are joined with Palestrina knot stitch to form a case for your thimble.

REQUIREMENTS

- Bronze silk — 25 cm x 25 cm (10" x 10")

- Calico/muslin — 25 cm x 25 cm (10" x 10")

- 20 cm (8") embroidery hoop

- Prepared cardboard shapes (see p.127)

- Plum/wine felt — 10 cm x 20 cm (4" x 8")

- Paper-backed fusible web

- Mill Hill Petite Beads — 42012 (royal plum)

- Mill Hill Petite Beads — 40161 (crystal)

- Hedgehog (see p. 85)

- Spider and web (see p. 118, 119)

- Tiny bee (see p.68)

- Threads: Dark green stranded (DMC 937 or Au Ver à Soie d'Alger 2126)
  Dark plum stranded (DMC 3802)
  Brown stranded cotton in three shades (DMC 610, 611, 612)

Brown silk thread in three shades (Cifonda 497, 498, 222)
Silver metallic (Madeira Metallic No. 40 — silver)
Bronze stranded (DMC 610, 611)

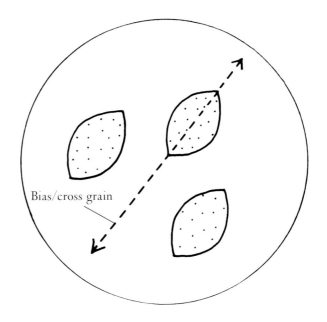

Bias/cross grain

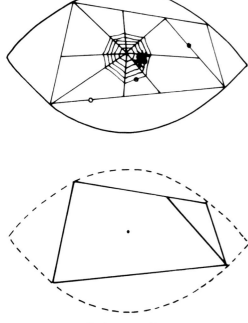

Skeleton outline

ORDER OF WORK

1.   Mount the silk and calico backing into the embroidery hoop. Using the cardboard shapes as templates, mark three pipkin outlines on the calico backing, placing the segments on the bias (cross) grain of the fabric with a space between each for a turning allowance. Tack/baste around the outlines with rayon machine thread.

2.   *Spider web segment* Trace the skeleton outline of the web onto the calico backing, inside the tacked segment. Work a spider web and spider within the segment outlines, using the tracing as a guide. Add crystal petite beads for dewdrops if desired.

3.   *Hedgehog segment* Trace the skeleton outline of the design onto the calico backing, inside the tacked segment. Embroider the hedgehog, using the tracing as a guide to placement.

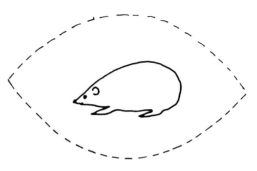

Skeleton outline

Work the grass in straight stitches with one strand of dark green thread, then embroider a tiny bee (see p.68).

4.   *Base segment* Trace the skeleton outline of the design onto the calico backing, inside the tacked segment. Thread trace the vine from the skeleton outline, then embroider in whipped chain stitch with dark green thread (937 or 2126), removing the tracing threads as you work. Starting at the base of the vine, work the chain stitch with two strands of thread to the first single leaf, then with one strand to the tip. Whip back down the vine with one strand of thread, then finish the base with a detached chain stitch. Work the small leaves with detached chain stitches, and the large leaf in padded satin stitch.

Hedgehog padding

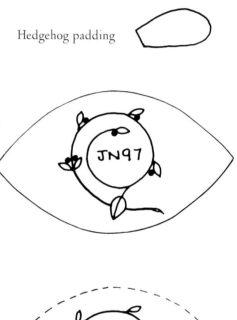

Using one strand of dark plum thread, apply the petite beads then backstitch the initials and the date.

TO COMPLETE THE THIMBLE PIPKIN

You will need:

— three prepared cardboard segments

— strong thread for gathering

— iron and pressing cloth (and/or GLAD Bake)

— plum/wine felt

— paper-backed fusible web

— bronze thread in a size 7 straw needle (two strands of 611 and one strand of 610).

Skeleton outline

1. Remove the paper backing (from the fusible web) from the other side of the prepared cardboard segments (see Step 4, p.127).

2. Cut out the embroidered pipkin shape, leave a 7mm ($\frac{1}{4}$") turning allowance outside the tacked/basted outline on the silk only — cut the calico backing close to the tacking. Run a row of gathering stitches within the silk allowance, using strong thread.

3. Gather the embroidery around one cardboard shape (pellon side against the calico backing), having the cardboard aligned with the tacked outline. Secure the gathering thread. Remove the tacking/basting. Trim and neaten the corners, then press the gathered turning allowance to flatten, (and fuse to the cardboard if using fusible web).

4. Repeat for the other two sides of the pipkin.

5. The pipkin is lined with the wine-coloured felt. Trace three segment shapes onto the paper side of the fusible web, then iron it on to the felt. Cut out the felt shapes, check for size and trim if necessary (they should be a shade smaller than the fabric covered cardboard), then remove the paper and fuse one to the back of each pipkin segment.

6. Work a row of Palestrina knot stitch across the top edge of both pipkin sides, catching in the edge of the felt. These edges will be the opening of the pipkin. Join the lower edge of the sides to the pipkin base with Palestrina knot stitch.

Note: To open your thimble case, gently squeeze the corners towards each other.

Scissors Scabbard

The front of the scabbard is decorated with a padded owl perched in a vine of beaded boysenberries; the back with a tiny soldier-fly. The scabbard pieces are joined with Palestrina knot stitch.

REQUIREMENTS

- Bronze silk:— 25 cm x 25 cm (10'' x 10'')
  — 25 cm x 15 cm (10'' x 6'') for lining

- Calico/muslin — 25 cm x 25 cm (10'' x 10'')

- 20 cm (8'') embroidery hoop

- Prepared cardboard shapes (see p.127)

- Boysenberries (see p.161)

- Owl (see p.65)

- Soldier-fly (see p.169)

- Thread: Dark green stranded (DMC 937 or Au Ver à Soie d'Alger 2126)
  Medium green stranded (DMC 469 or Au Ver à Soie d'Alger 2125)
  Bronze stranded (DMC 610, 611)

ORDER OF WORK

1.   Mount the square of silk and calico backing into the embroidery hoop. Using the cardboard shapes as templates, mark one front and one back scabbard shape on to the calico backing, leaving at least 3 cm (1 ¼'') between the shapes to allow for turnings. Tack/baste around the shape lines with rayon machine thread.

Front skeleton outline

Scabbard front

2.   Trace the skeleton outline of the design on to the calico backing then thread-trace the vine outline (see p. 129). Work the vine in whipped chain stitch in dark green thread, using two strands for the vine and one strand for the berry stems. Remove the tracing threads as you work.

3.   The leaves are worked with one strand of dark green thread. Outline with small backstitches, using the traced outline on the calico backing as a guide, then embroider in padded satin stitch.

4.   Embroider the owl then apply to scabbard front, using the traced outline on the calico backing as a guide.

5.   Work three boysenberries, one at the end of each stem. Embroider three detached chain stitches at the base of each berry to form the sepals, using one strand of medium green thread.

Scabbard back

6.   Transfer the soldier-fly outline to the calico backing.

Work the soldier-fly (see p.169) using the outline on the calico as a guide.

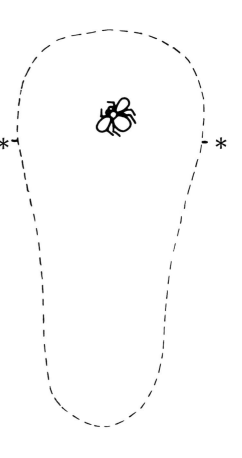

TO COMPLETE THE SCISSORS SCABBARD

You will need:

— prepared cardboard scabbard pieces (front, front lining, back and back lining)

— strong thread for gathering

— iron and pressing cloth (and/or GLAD Bake)

— PVA glue

— bronze thread in a size 7 straw needle (two strands of 611 and one strand of 610).

1.   Remove the paper backing (from the fusible web) from the other side of the prepared cardboard scabbard shapes (see Step 4, p.127).

2.   Cut out the embroidered front scabbard shape, leave a 1 cm ($1/2$'') turning allowance outside the tacked/basted outline on the silk only — cut the calico backing close to the tacking. Run a row of gathering stitches within the silk allowance, using strong thread.

3.   Gather the embroidery around the front scabbard cardboard shape (place the pellon side against the calico backing), having the cardboard aligned with the tacked outline. Secure the gathering thread. Remove the tacking/basting. Trim and neaten the corners, then press the gathered turning allowance to flatten (and fuse to the cardboard if using fusible web).

4.   Repeat for the scabbard back.

5.   Mark both scabbard lining shapes onto the back of the lining silk, leaving at least 3 cm (1 and $1/4$'') between shapes

to allow for turnings. Cut out the shapes leaving a 1 cm ($^1\!/_2$'')
seam allowance. Gather the lining around the prepared cardboard lining shapes, placing the pellon side against the silk.
Secure the gathering thread. Trim and neaten the corners, then
press the gathered turning allowance to flatten (and fuse to
the cardboard if using fusible web).

6.   Glue the front and front lining, and back and back lining
together, making sure that the top edges between * and * are
even, and using a minimal amount of glue. Place the glued
shapes on a soft towelling pad (embroidered side down), and
press under books until dry.

7.   Work a row of Palestrina knot stitch across the top edge
of each scabbard piece between * and * (catching the scabbard
piece and its lining together). These edges will be the opening
of the scabbard. Join the scabbard shapes together around the
lower edge between * and * with Palestrina knot stitch, securing the stitches well at *.

Needlebook

A padded squirrel with a velvety tail is embroidered on the front of the needlebook; a beehive with tiny bees on the back. The needlebook has leaves of wool flannel or felt.

REQUIREMENTS

- Bronze silk — 25 cm x 25 cm (10" x 10")

- Calico/muslin — 25 cm x 25 cm (10" x 10")

- 20 cm (8") embroidery hoop

- Prepared cardboard shapes (see p.127)

- Cream woollen doctor flannel or felt

- Beehive (see p.67)

- Squirrel (see p.170)

- Tiny bees (see p.68)

- Threads: Olive green chenille
  Dark green stranded (DMC 937 or Au Ver à Soie d'Alger 2126)
  Bronze stranded (DMC 610, 611)
  Bronze machine thread (to match silk)

ORDER OF WORK

1.   Mount the silk and calico backing into the embroidery hoop. Draw the needlecase outline onto the backing and tack/baste around these lines with rayon machine thread.

2.   Trace the skeleton outline of the design onto the calico backing, inside the tacked outline (see p.129).

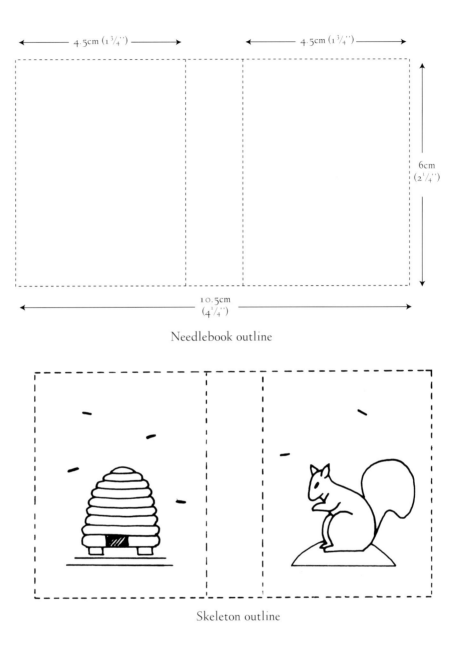

Needlebook outline

Skeleton outline

3. *Needlebook front.* With one strand of dark green thread, outline the mound under the squirrel with backstitch (following the outline on the calico backing). Fill the mound with rows of couched chenille thread, starting at * and ending in the centre of the mound. Use one strand of dark green thread to couch the chenille and to secure the chenille thread ends at the back of the work.

Note: If chenille thread is unavailable, work the mound in Turkey knots using two strands of dark green thread.

Work the squirrel (see p.171) over the mound, using the tracing as a guide to placement.

4.   *Needlebook back.* Referring to the tracing on the back for placement, work the beehive (see p.67) using only one layer of felt for padding (top layer). Stitch the legs at the base of the beehive in satin stitch with one strand of dark gold thread (680). For grass, couch two rows of chenille thread at the base of the beehive. Use one strand of dark green thread to couch the chenille and to secure the chenille thread ends at the back of the work.

Note: If chenille thread is unavailable, work the grass in Turkey knots using two strands of the dark green thread.

5.   Tiny bees (see p.68). Work tiny bees on the front and the back of the needlebook.

TO COMPLETE THE NEEDLEBOOK

You will need:

— Two prepared cardboard rectangles (see p.127)

— Iron

— Ruler and pencil (or fine marking pen)

— Machine thread to match the silk

— Cream woollen doctor flannel or felt — two pieces 6 cm x
    10 cm (2³⁄₈'' x 4'')

— Bronze thread in a size 7 straw needle (two strands of 611
    and one strand of 610).

1.   Remove the needlebook embroidery from the hoop and iron lightly on the back to flatten the edges.

2.   Rule the following lines on to the calico backing to form the needlebook pattern:
— 2 mm (³⁄₁₆'') away from the upper and lower edges of the needlebook outline (these lines become the stitching lines on the upper and lower edges).
— 2 mm (³⁄₁₆'') away from the side edges of the needlebook outline (these lines become the fold lines on the side edges).

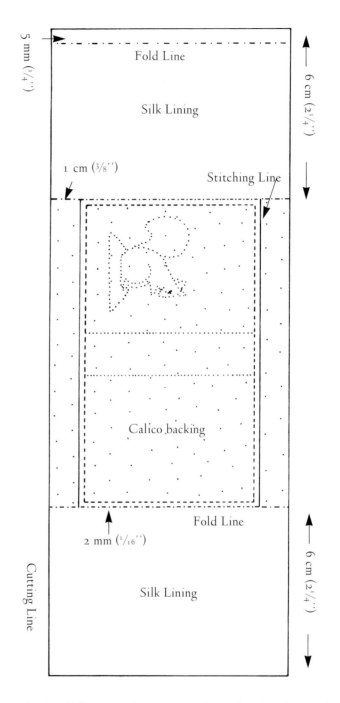

3. Rule the following lines on to the calico backing, then cut the calico (and the silk) along these lines
— 1 cm (³⁄₈'') away from the upper and lower stitching lines (this becomes the seam allowance).
— 6 cm (2³⁄₈'') away from the fold lines on each side edge (this will become the lining of the needlebook).

4.   To reduce bulk, cut the 6 cm (2 ½'') calico lining section away close to the fold lines on each side, leaving a silk lining only. On the side edge of the silk front lining (squirrel side), press a 5 mm (³/₈'') seam allowance to the wrong side.

5.   With right sides facing, fold the front lining along the fold line (over the squirrel), then fold the back lining along the fold line (the back lining will overlap the front lining). Pin the edges together, making sure that the upper and lower edges are even.

Cross-section

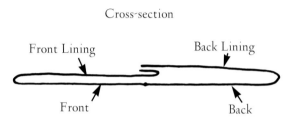

6.   With the calico side up, stitch the upper and lower edges of the needlebook along the stitching lines 1 cm (½'') from the edge. Trim seams. Cut calico close to stitching and reduce silk seam allowance to 5 mm (³/₈'').

7.   Turn the back of the needlebook to the right side through the central opening and insert one cardboard shape (pellon side towards calico). Then turn the front of the needle-book to the right side and insert the remaining cardboard shape. Ease the cardboard shapes into the corners of the needlebook, then close the opening with slip stitches. (Trim the cardboard shapes to fit if necessary).

8.   Trim the edges of the flannel pieces with pinking or scal-loping shears. Place both pieces of flannel inside the needle-book to form pages for needles and back stitch all layers together down the centre fold with machine thread. Work a row of Palestrina knot stitch (with bronze stranded thread) on the spine of the needlebook to cover these back stitches. Trim the flannel page edges with shears, if necessary.

Embroidered Pouch

Each surface of this pouch, which can be used to carry your needlework accessories, is embroidered with a garland of beaded boysenberries enclosing a spider web and spider on one side, and your initials on the other. Beaded berries are worked at the ends of twisted cords to form the drawstrings. The pouch can also be used as an evening bag. Work a smaller version, perhaps in creams, for a jewellery pouch or as a beautiful wrapping for a gift.

REQUIREMENTS

Note: It is important to cut the fabrics accurately as the measurements form the pattern for the pouch.

- Bronze silk — 2 rectangles 50 cm x 25 cm (20" x 10")

- Calico/muslin — 2 squares 25 cm x 25 cm (10" x 10")

- Thin wadding (Pellon) — 2 squares 25 cm x 25 cm (10" x 10")

- 20 cm (8") embroidery hoop

- Plum/wine felt — small piece

- Mill Hill Frosted Glass Beads — 62056 (boysenberry)

- Mill Hill Frosted Glass Beads — 60367 (garnet)

- Mill Hill Glass Seed Beads — 367 (garnet)

- Mill Hill Petite Beads — 40161 (crystal)

- 1 m (40") purchased dark green twisted cord or two skeins of green stranded thread (DMC 937) to make your own.

- Boysenberries (see p.161)

- Tiny bees (see p.68)

- Threads: Dark green stranded (DMC 937 or Au Ver à Soie d'Alger 2126)
  Medium green stranded (DMC 469 or Au Ver à Soie d'Alger 2125)
  Deep red stranded (DMC 815 or Au Ver à Soie d'Alger 2926)
  Silver metallic (Madeira Metallic No.40 silver) for web

ORDER OF WORK

Preparation

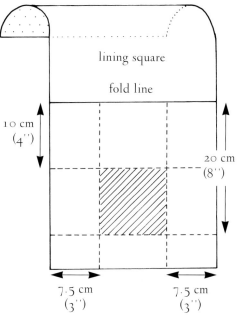

lining square

calico
pellon } fabric sandwich
silk

fold

Cross-section of fabric sandwich

1.   Fold one piece of silk in half (wrong sides together) to form a 25 cm (10") square and press the fold. Unfold the silk and place one half over a pellon and a calico square to form a fabric sandwich. Pin then tack/baste the three layers together around all edges of the square. The remaining half of the silk will form the lining of the pouch.

2.   Using a ruler and lead pencil, draw the following lines on the calico side of the fabric sandwich (edge tacking lines are not shown).
— 10 cm (4") from the fold line
— 20 cm (8") from the fold line
— 7.5 cm (3") from each side

lining square

fold line

10 cm
(4")

20 cm
(8")

7.5 cm
(3")

7.5 cm
(3")

3. Tack around the central 10 cm (4'') square formed by these lines.

4. Mount the fabric sandwich in a 20 cm (8'') hoop, silk side up, taking care to keep the basted square 'square'. (Fabric needs to be firm but it is not necessary to be drum tight). Trace the skeleton outline onto the calico backing — centring the design within the tacked square. Take care to place the design so that it will be the right way round on the silk upper layer.

Repeat this procedure with the remaining fabrics for the other side of the pouch.

Skeleton outline for both
sides of the pouch

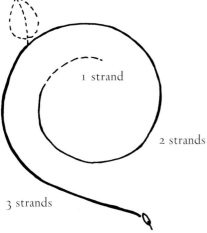

1 strand

2 strands

3 strands

5. *Vine.* Thread trace the vine outline, then embroider in whipped chain stitch with dark green thread (937 or 2126), removing the tracing threads as you work. Starting at the base, work the chain stitch with three strands of thread to the first single leaf, two strands of thread until 1 ½ cm (¾'') from the end, then one strand to the end of the stem. Whip back down the stem with one strand of thread, then finish the base with a detached chain stitch.

6.   *Leaves.* The large leaves are embroidered with one strand of dark green thread as follows:
— work the central veins and stalks in chain stitch
— outline each leaf in backstitch, using the traced outline on the calico backing as a guide
— pad the leaf surface with straight stitches
— embroider each side of the leaf with close buttonhole stitches, the buttonholed edge just covering the backstitch outline.

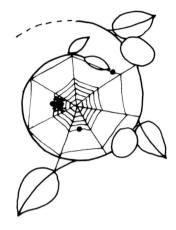

Outline the small leaves with backstitch, then embroider in padded satin stitch.

7.   *Boysenberries* (see p.161)

Work three detached chain stitches at the base of each berry to form the sepals, using one strand of medium green thread (DMC 469 or Au Ver à Soie d'Alger 2125).

8.   Spider web and spider (see p. 118, 119 ). Add crystal petite beads for dewdrops if desired.

9.   Using the alphabet provided, work initials in chain stitch using one strand of deep red thread (DMC 815 or Au Ver à Soie d'Alger 2926).

10.   Tiny Bees (see p.68) are worked where desired on each side of the pouch.

$$A \quad B \quad C \quad D \quad E \quad F \quad G$$
$$H \quad I \quad J \quad K \quad L \quad M \quad N$$
$$O \quad P \quad Q \quad R \quad S \quad T \quad U$$
$$V \quad W \quad X \quad Y \quad Z$$

TO COMPLETE THE POUCH

PREPARE BOTH SIDES OF THE POUCH AS FOLLOWS:

1.   Remove the fabric sandwich from the hoop and draw the following lines on the calico backing (see Construction Lines diagram on page 153):

(a) 2.5 cm (1'') and 4 cm (1½'') from the fold — these are the casing lines.

(b) 3 cm (1⅛'') from the fold — tack/baste this line to keep the three layers in place when stitching the casing.

(c) 5 cm (2'') from each side — round the corners of these lines (I used a 10 cm, 4'' tin as a template). These lines (with their rounded corners) are the stitching lines for the pouch.

2.   Cut away 3.5 cm (1⅜'') from all edges of the silk (both the sandwich and the lining) to leave a 1.5cm (⅝'') seam allowance. Round all the corners as above.

MACHINE STITCH THE POUCH (WITH MATCHING THREAD) AS FOLLOWS:

3.   With right sides facing and matching the fold lines, pin both sides of the pouch and pouch lining together around the outside edge (insert the pins at right-angles to the seam line and remove as you stitch). Beginning and ending securely, machine stitch around the outside edge of the pouch, with a seam allowance of 1.5 cm (⅝'') for the padded section of the pouch, and 1.8 cm (¾'') for the pouch lining. Leave openings between the casing lines and for 5 cm (2'') at the lower edge of the lining (between the large dots • on the diagram).

4.   Trim the seam allowance then turn the pouch to the right side through the opening in the lining. Finger press the seams then slip stitch the lining opening closed. Ease the lining inside the pouch and press along the fold.

5.   To form a casing for the drawstrings, machine stitch 2.5 cm (1'') and 4 cm (1½'') from the top edge (fold). Remove the tacking/basting threads. The casing should coincide with the openings at the sides to allow for the insertion of the cords.

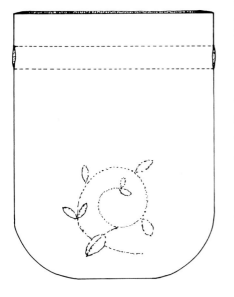

Make two twisted cords as follows:

6.   Use one skein 8 m (8 yards) of stranded thread (DMC 937) for each cord:

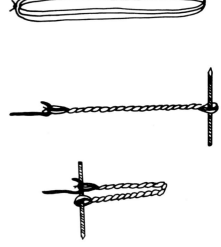

   (a) Unwind the skein of thread and fold into six equal lengths. Knot the ends.

   (b) Loop one end of threads over a pencil and the other end over a hook. Keeping the threads taut, twist the pencil round and round until the threads begin to twist on themselves.

   (c) Holding the cord firmly, fold in half and the cords will twist together. Whip the ends together then trim off any uneven ends or previous knots.

   or Cut the bought cord into two 50 cm lengths.

7   Thread both cords through the casing, having each cord beginning and ending on opposite sides of the pouch.

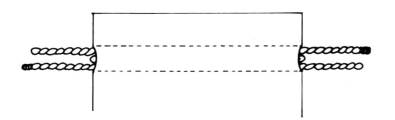

8.   Work a detached beaded boysenberry (see p.162) at the ends of each cord.

9.   Using one strand of matching green thread, stitch then wrap the cord ends together about 1.5 cm (⅝'') above the berries.

CONSTRUCTION LINES FOR POUCH

Diagrams not to scale

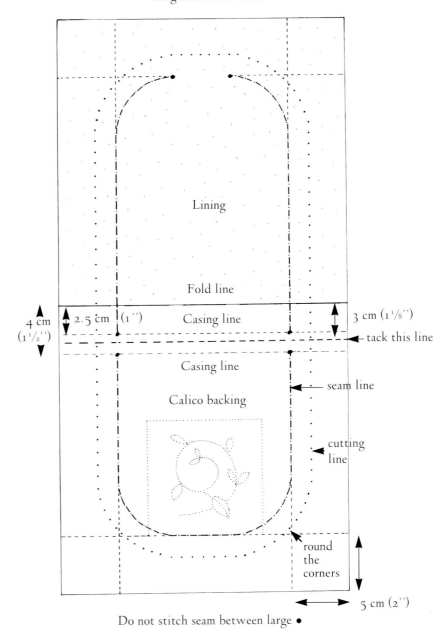

OUTLINES FOR SMALLER POUCHES

Use your own choice of threads and beads

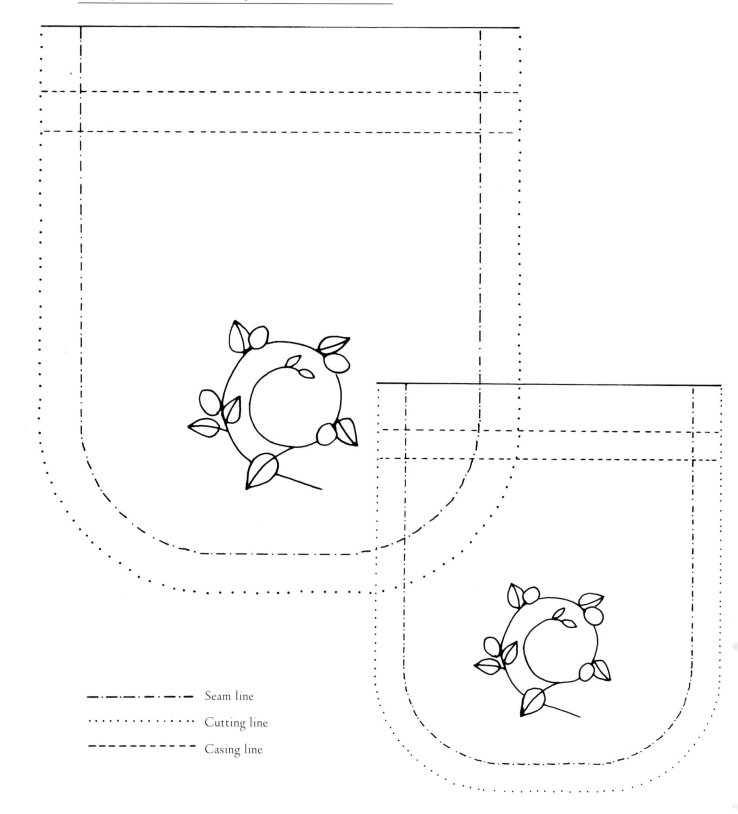

—·—·—·—·— Seam line

·············· Cutting line

— — — — — Casing line

Walnut Pincushion

A walnut pincushion makes a charming gift or attach a fine gold cord and hang it on your Christmas tree. This tiny project can also be mounted into a small oval frame or pendant.

REQUIREMENTS

- Ivory or bronze silk — 15 cm x 15 cm (6'' x 6'')

- Calico (or quilter's muslin) — 15 cm x 15 cm (6'' x 6'')

- Red homespun — 15 cm x 15 cm (6'' x 6'')

- 10 cm (4'') embroidery hoops

- Walnut shell (halved)

- Wire — fine flower wire in 12 cm (5'') length

- Red marking pen to colour wire if desired

- Stuffing (wool or polyester)

- Mill Hill Frosted Glass Beads — 62056 (boysenberry)

- Mill Hill Frosted Glass Beads — 60367 (garnet)

- Mill Hill Glass Seed Beads — 367 (garnet)

- Mill Hill Petite Beads — 42014 (black)

- Needles: Crewel/embroidery 10
  Sharps/Appliqué 12
  Large yarn darner or chenille 18

- Thread: Dark green stranded (DMC 937)
  Medium green stranded (DMC 469)
  Dark purple/plum stranded (Au Ver à Soie d'Alger 3326
  or DMC 902)
  Red stranded (DMC 349)
  Black stranded (DMC 310)

ORDER OF WORK

1.   Mount the silk and calico backing into the embroidery hoop and mark the cutting line. Trace the skeleton outline, inside the marked oval, indicating the centre of the boysenberries with a short line (3mm or ⅛'').

2.   *Stems.* Using one strand of dark green thread, embroider the stems in stem stitch. Work one row to each berry (two rows side by side at the base) and to each leaf.

3.   *Leaves.* Embroider the leaves in fishbone stitch with one strand of dark green thread.

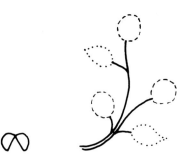

4.   *Boysenberries* (see p.161). Work three detached chain stitches at the base of each berry for sepals, using one strand of medium green thread.

5.   *Tiny ladybird* (see p.37). Using the wing size shown on the design outline.

6.   Remove the embroidery from the hoop and cut along the marked oval. Trim calico backing layer to an oval shape along the calico cutting line. Run a gathering thread around the outside edge, insert a tight wad of stuffing (it takes more than imagined!), then pull up the gathering thread and secure. Force the shape into the walnut shell, easing the gathers around the edges. A little PVA glue can be used in the base of the walnut shell if desired. This embroidery can also be mounted in a small oval frame or pendant.

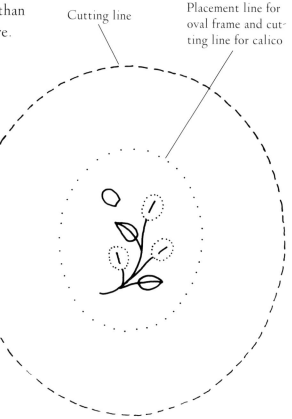

Cutting line

Placement line for oval frame and cutting line for calico

Skeleton outline

Stumpwork Name Brooch

Other fruits and insects could be substituted to produce your own version of this stumpwork name brooch.

MATERIALS REQUIRED

- Ivory/gold satin — 2 squares, 20 cm x 20 cm (8'' x 8'')
- Calico (or quilter's muslin) — 20 cm x 20 cm (8'' x 8'')
- 10 cm (4'') embroidery hoop
- Dark green stranded thread (DMC 937 or Au Ver à Soie d'Alger 2126)
- Acorn (see p. 35 )
- Grapes (see p. 83)
- Pomegranate (see p. 104)
- Red currants (see p. 68)
- Small snail (see p. 116)
- Mill Hill Antique Beads 3014 (olive)

JANE NICHOLAS

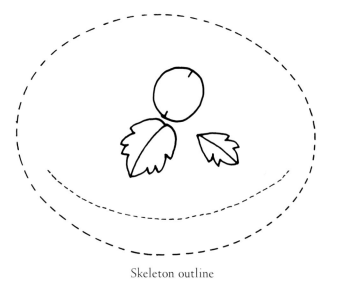

Pomegranate template

Skeleton outline

ORDER OF WORK

1.   Mount the satin and calico backing into the embroidery hoop. Using the cardboard shape as a template, mark the brooch outline on to the calico backing. Tack/baste around the outline with rayon machine thread.

2.   Trace the skeleton outline of the design onto the calico backing, inside the tacked oval (see p.129).

3.   The leaves are embroidered with one strand of dark green thread as follows:
— work the central veins in chain stitch
— outline each leaf in backstitch, using the traced outline on the calico backing as a guide
— pad the leaf surface with straight stitches
— embroider each side of the leaf with satin stitch (covering the outline).

4.   Pomegranate.

5.   Grapes.

6.   Acorn.

7.   Red currants.

8.   Small snail.

9.   *Initials.* Using the alphabet provided, work the initials in back stitch with one strand of dark green thread , then whip with a fine gold thread.

ALPHABET FOR NAME BROOCH

A B C D E F G H I J K L M N O P Q R S T U V W X Y Z

TO COMPLETE THE NAME BROOCH

You will need:
— two ovals of 1mm cardboard (the size of the brooch)
— pellon and fusible web
— strong thread
— brooch pin
— glass seed beads for edging

1.   Prepare two oval cardboard shapes (see p.127, steps 3 and 4). Remove the paper backing (from the fusible web) from the other side of the prepared cardboard ovals.

2.   Cut out the embroidered oval with a 1.5 cm (³/₄'') turning allowance. Run a row of gathering stitches within this allowance, using strong thread.

3.   Gather the embroidery around one cardboard oval (pellon side against the calico backing), having the cardboard aligned with the tacked outline. Secure the gathering thread and work a few lacing stitches. Remove the tacking. Press the gathered turning allowance to flatten (and fuse to the cardboard if using fusible web).

4.   Cut an oval of satin and gather over the remaining cardboard, as above, for the brooch back. Attach a brooch pin to the back by stitching through the fabric and the cardboard.

5.   Stitch the front oval to the back oval with invisible slip stitches (ladder stitch), making sure that the brooch pin is in the correct position.

6.   To make a bead edging, thread on to one strand of strong thread enough seed beads to fit snugly around the circumference of the brooch. Tie the thread into a circle around the edge of the brooch, allowing the beads to rest in the groove formed between the two ovals of cardboard. Slip stitch the strong thread in place between every three or four beads.

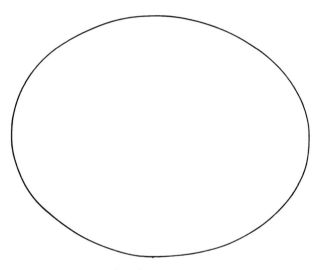

Template for cardboard oval

Needlework Accessories

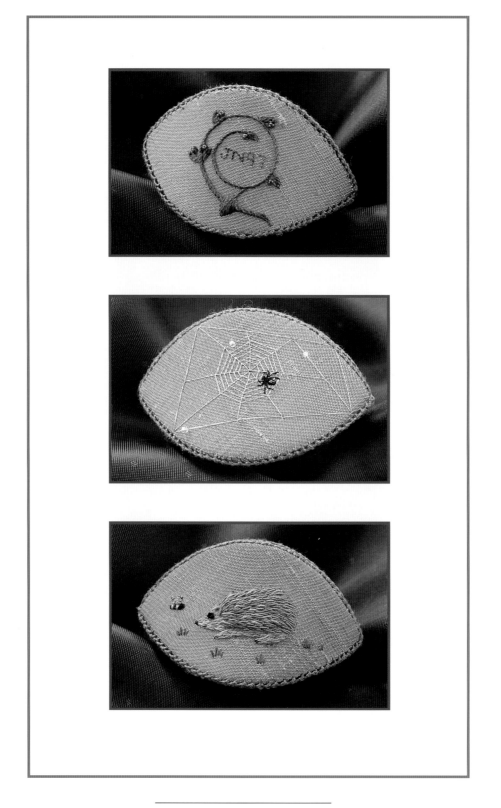

THIMBLE PIPKIN (sides and base)

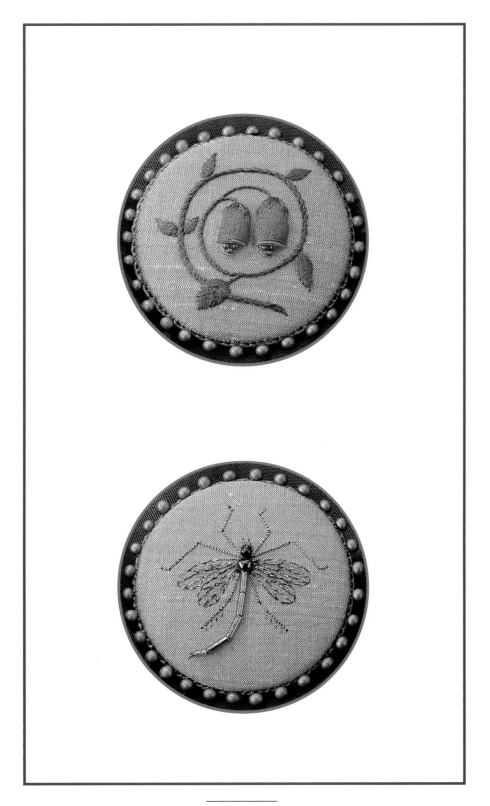

PIN WHEEL

SCISSORS SCABBARD

NEEDLEBOOK *(front)*

NEEDLEBOOK *(back)*

ACCESSORIES POUCH (*back*)

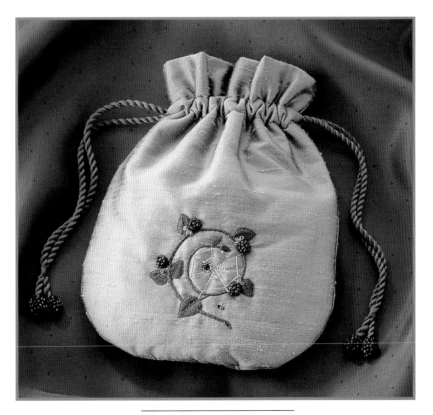

ACCESSORIES POUCH (*front*)

STUMPWORK NAME BROOCH

Walnut Pincushion

BOYSENBERRY PENDANT

Boysenberries

MATERIALS REQUIRED

- Beads: Mill Hill Frosted Glass Beads 62056 (boysenberry)
  Mill Hill Frosted Glass Beads 60367 (garnet)
  Mill Hill Glass Seed Beads 367 (garnet)

- Plum/purple felt — small piece

- Needles: Crewel/embroidery 10

- Thread: Dark purple/plum stranded (Au Ver à Soie d'Alger 3326 or DMC 902)

BOYSENBERRIES ON FABRIC

1. Mark the centre of the berries with a short line, 3mm (¹/₈''). The berries are formed by stitching beads to the main fabric, in two layers as shown, using one strand of purple/plum thread. Apply the beads one at a time and mix the colours as desired.

Lower layer

a.   Stitch two beads on the centre line.

b.   Backstitch nine beads around the centre then run three rounds of thread through these beads to draw them into a tight oval (as if threading a necklace).

Upper layer

c.   Stitch one bead in the centre (take the needle between the beads in the lower layer through to the back).

d.   Back stitch seven beads around the centre then run three rounds of thread through these beads to draw them into a tight oval. Secure the thread at the back.

2.   *Sepals* — see individual instructions, e.g. point 7, page 150.

Detatched Beaded Boysenberries

The boysenberry, a variety of trailing blackberry, belongs to the rose family, Rosaceae. This dark, shiny reddish-black berry is rather soft and has a tart flavour.

These boysenberries can be worked as cord ends for a drawstring bag, or, when worked over padding, can be applied as detached berries to an embroidery.

MATERIALS REQUIRED

- Beads: Mill Hill Frosted Glass Beads 62056 (boysenberry)
  Mill Hill Frosted Glass Beads 60367 (garnet)
  Mill Hill Glass Seed Beads 367 (garnet)

- 3 mm (1/8'') twisted cord (made or purchased) for drawstrings

- Plum/purple felt — 8 mm (1/3'') strip to wind around the ends of the cords.

- Needles: Crewel/embroidery 10
  Darning 18

- Thread: Dark purple/plum stranded (DMC 902 or Au Ver à Soie d'Alger 3326)
  Dark green stranded (DMC 937 or Au Ver à Soie d'Alger 2126)
  Dark green soft cotton (DMC Tapestry Cotton 2936)

Preparation for cord (drawstring) ends

1. Cut the cord to the required length and wrap the cut ends with green stranded cotton to prevent unravelling.

Note: Insert the cords through the casing before working the berries.

2. Wind one layer of felt around each end of the cords and secure with a few stitches.

Preparation for detached berries to apply to embroidery

1. Cut a strip of felt, 2.5 cm x 8 mm (1″ x 5/16″), and a 30 cm (12″) length of soft cotton.

2. Using one strand of plum/purple thread, stitch one short end of the felt to the middle of the length of soft cotton. Roll the felt around the soft cotton core to form a cylinder and stitch the other short end to secure.

3. Insert the darning needle through the core of the cylinder (this makes it easier to hold when applying the beads to form the berry).

To work the berries

Use one strand of plum/purple thread to stitch the beads to the felt base, selecting the colours at random. Each bead is applied with a backstitch, which goes through the previous bead as follows:

(a) Bring the needle up at 1, back through the bead, then down at 2.

(b) Bring the needle up at 3, back through two beads, then down at 2.

(c) Bring the needle up at 4, back through two beads, then down at 1.

(d) Bring the needle up at 5, back through two beads, then down at 3 and so on.

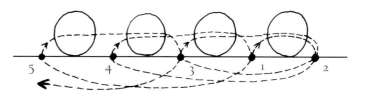

Each berry has six rows of beads:

Rows 1 and 2: Backstitch two rows of beads around the centre of the felt (12 beads in each row). Run a thread through each row of beads to form a smooth circle.

Rows 3 and 4: Rows 3 and 4 are stitched at the same time (to avoid a gap occurring). Using backstitch as above to apply each bead, stitch bead 1 in Row 3, then slip the needle through the felt to stitch bead 1 in Row 4. Slip the needle through the felt to stitch bead 2 in Row 3, then slip the needle through the felt to stitch bead 2 in Row 4, and so on until all beads are applied (10 beads in each row). Run a thread through each row of beads to draw together smoothly into a circle.

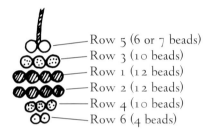

Row 5 (6 or 7 beads)
Row 3 (10 beads)
Row 1 (12 beads)
Row 2 (12 beads)
Row 4 (10 beads)
Row 6 (4 beads)

Rows 5 and 6: Rows 5 and 6 are stitched at the same time, slipping the needle through the felt between each row as above. Stitch 7 beads (Row 5) around the cord at the top of the berry (use 6 beads if using soft cotton) and at the same time stitch 4 beads to form the base of the berry (Row 6). Run a thread through Row 5 to draw the beads into a circle. Secure the thread.

Note: If working detached berries to apply to embroidery, thread the soft cotton from the lower end of the berry into the darning needle, and pull through to the top of the berry before stitching Rows 5 and 6. Trim this thread close to the felt (the remaining thread will be wrapped to form a stalk). When the berry is complete, wrap the soft cotton thread with one strand of dark green thread to the desired length to form a stalk. Secure.

Dragonfly

MATERIALS REQUIRED:

- Bronze organza — 10 cm x 10 cm (4'' x 4'')

- Gold metal organdie — 10 cm x 10 cm (4'' x 4'')

- Paper-backed fusible web — 10 cm x 10 cm (4'' x 4''), and another small piece

- Beads: Eyes — Mill Hill Petite Beads 40374 (teal)
  Head — 4 mm teal bead (Hotspotz SBXL – 449)
  Thorax — 6 mm teal bead (Hotspotz SBX6 – 449)
  Abdomen — Mill Hill Small Bugle Beads 72053 (nutmeg)
  — Mill Hill Petite Beads 42024 (nutmeg)

- Needles: Straw/milliners 9
  Sharps/Appliqué 12

- Threads: Bronze/black metallic (Kreinik Cord 215c)
  Peacock-green metallic filament (Kreinik Blending
  Filament colour 085)
  Nylon clear thread

Note: Thread trace the dragonfly head, thorax and abdomen from the skeleton outline, using rayon machine thread.

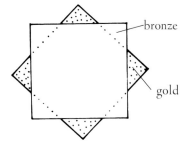

bronze

gold

Dragonfly wings

1. Prepare the wing sandwich by fusing the bronze organza and the gold organdie together using paper-backed fusible web. A pretty effect is gained by applying one layer of fabric on the cross-grain.

2. Trace the wing outlines (from the skeleton outline) onto the paper side of the remaining piece of fusible web and iron to the gold side of the wing sandwich (the bronze side is the right side of the wing sandwich). Carefully cut out the wing shapes. Remove the paper backing and fuse the wing shapes in position on the silk, using a piece of GLAD Bake to protect the wings and the iron. (Use pins inserted from the back along

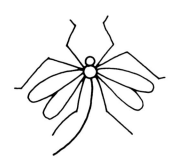

skeleton outline

the traced lines to indicate the wing positions — remove
before you iron).

3. With the blending filament in the straw needle and the
nylon thread in the sharps needle, couch a line of blending filament around the outside edge of each wing, using the nylon
thread to work the couching stitches (stitch *from* the silk *towards*
the wing to prevent the wing edge lifting). Using the blending
filament, work the veins of the wings in feather stitch.

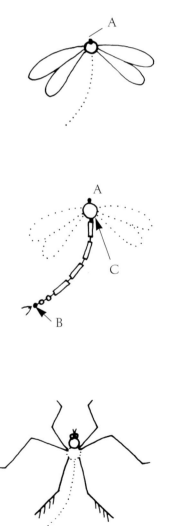

diagram not to scale

Dragonfly body

Note: The beads for body of the dragonfly are applied with
one strand of bronze/black metallic thread in the sharps needle. Remove the tracing threads as you work.

1. *Thorax.* Bring the needle up at A and stitch the 6mm bead
in place with two vertical straight stitches over the thorax
(where all the wings join).

2. *Abdomen.* Bring the needle up at A (and through the thorax bead), then thread on 4 bugle beads and 2 petite beads
(nutmeg) and insert the needle at B (make sure the length of
the stitch is longer than the combined length of the beads so
that the beads will sit smoothly). Bring the needle up at C,
then couch between each bead back to B, removing the tracing
thread as you go. Work a fly stitch for the tail and bring the
tie-down thread back through all the beads to A (you may
need tweezers to pull the short needle through).

3. *Head.* Bring the needle up at A and apply the 4mm bead
for the head. To work the eyes, apply two petite beads
together (with a straight stitch from side to side), close to the
head. Finish with one stitch between the beads towards the
head — this makes the beads sit together.

4. *Legs.* With two strands of the bronze/black metallic
thread in the straw needle, work three back stitches for each
leg, using the traced outline on the calico backing as a guide.
With one strand of thread, work straight stitches for the
hairs on the back legs and a fly stitch for the feelers.

Foxgloves

MATERIALS REQUIRED

- Calico (or quilter's muslin) — 20 cm x 20 cm (8'' x 8'')

- 10 cm (4'') embroidery hoop

- Wire: Fine flower wire, cut in 12 cm (5'') lengths

- Small amount of stuffing and a saté stick (optional)

- Mill Hill Petite Beads 42012 (royal plum)

- Needles: Crewel/embroidery 10
  Chenille 18
  Sharps 12 (or beading needle)

- Threads: Dark green stranded (DMC 937 or Au Ver à Soie d'Alger 2126)
  Dark pink stranded (DMC 309 or Au Ver à Soie d'Alger 2934)
  Medium pink stranded (DMC 335 or Au Ver à Soie d'Alger 2933)

To embroider the upper foxglove shapes

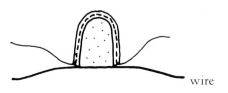

wire

1. Mount the calico into the hoop and trace the upper fox-glove outlines, enlarging them slightly at the sides and top edge to allow for the raised shape.

2. Couch, then buttonhole stitch the wire to the calico along the lower edge with the medium pink thread (leaving the tails of wire free), then work a row of long and short but-tonhole stitch close to the wire. Using one strand of dark pink thread, embroider the remainder of the shape in long and short stitch.

3. Make a row of running stitches 1 mm away from the sides and top of the embroidered shape, leaving thread tails at each side. Carefully cut out the flower shape, leaving a small turning around the outside edge and cutting close to the wire at the lower edge (do not cut off the wire or thread tails).

To apply upper foxglove shape to main fabric

1. With one strand of medium pink thread, outline the fox-glove shapes (on the main fabric) in backstitch, using the traced outline on the calico backing as a guide. Work the lower edge of the foxglove shapes in long and short button-hole stitch, covering the lower third of the shape.

2. To apply the embroidered shape, gently pull the thread tails to ease the turning to the inside. Position the top of the shape at the end of the stem with a stab stitch, then, using a chenille needle, insert the wires at the lower points • and secure at the back of the work. Stab stitch the outside edge in place along the outline, gently pulling the thread tails to ease the shape to size. Cut the thread tails. Cover the stab stitches with straight stitches in blending colours, if required. A little stuffing can be inserted into each foxglove to maintain the shape when the pin wheel is used.

3. Using two strands of dark green thread, embroider four detached chain stitches at the top of each flower to form the sepals. Use a saté stick to gently raise and shape the upper layer of the foxglove.

4. Complete by stitching three petite beads in the throat of each foxglove.

Soldier Fly

MATERIALS REQUIRED

- Gold organza ribbon (or scrap of wing sandwich from dragonfly wings)

- Paper-backed fusible web

- Mill Hill Petite Glass Beads 40374 (blue/black)

- Thread: Dark orange stranded (DMC 919 or Au Ver à Soie d'Alger 616)
  Peacock-green metallic filament (Kreinik Blending Filament colour 085)
  Bronze/black metallic thread (Kreinik Cord 215c)
  Bronze chenille thread

- Needles: Straw 9
  Crewel 10
  Sharps/Appliqué 12
  Chenille 18

Wings

1. Trace the wing outline on to the paper side of the paper-backed fusible web and iron to the back of the wing fabric. Carefully cut out the wing shape, remove the paper backing, then fuse the wing to the main fabric (protect with GLAD Bake). Couch a line of peacock blending filament around the wings, using another length of blending filament (in a straw needle) to work the couching stitches, then work a fly stitch in each wing for the veins.

Body

2. Work one or two stitches with chenille thread between the wings to form the thorax. Using one strand of dark orange thread, outline the abdomen with small backstitches, pad stitch, then satin stitch across the abdomen, covering the backstitches. Apply two petite beads for eyes. Embroider the legs in straight stitches with two strands of bronze metallic thread in a straw needle.

Squirrel

The European red squirrel has a large bushy tail and tufted ears that lighten before each moult. The summer coat of rich chestnut red fades to dull brown in winter. The last strongholds of this endangered species are pine forests, where they feed on conifer shoots and cones, chewing off the cone scales to remove the seeds.

MATERIALS REQUIRED

- Cream felt, paper-backed fusible web and silk organza — 8 cm x 5 cm (3'' x 2'')

- Eyebrow brush/comb

- Mill Hill Glass Seed Bead — 221 (bronze)

- Mill Hill Petite Bead — 42014 (black)

- Needles: Crewel/embroidery 5-10
  Sharps 12 (or beading needle)

- Threads: Dark brown stranded (DMC 3371)
  Shades of medium to light tan (DMC 434, 435, 436, 738, 739)
  Brown/grey stranded (DMC 3022)

1.   Iron the fusible web to the organza (protect the iron and ironing board with GLAD Bake). On the organza side, trace the squirrel body and all internal lines (not the tail or the back ear), and two successively smaller shapes for padding. Remove the paper and fuse the organza to the felt. Cut the shapes out carefully.

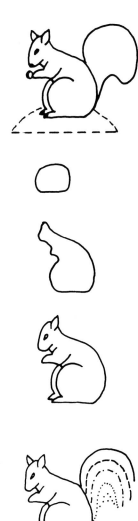

2. With one strand of light tan thread, stab stitch the three layers of felt in place, starting with the smallest shape and keeping the organza side uppermost (using the mound and the back tracing as a guide to placement). Outline the squirrel shape with buttonhole stitch around the top layer of felt.

3. Stitch along the internal lines with small stab stitches to sculpt the squirrel body, then, using the internal lines as a guide, embroider the squirrel in long and short stitch. Work in the following order with one strand of the suggested colours, to achieve the desired shading.

> Belly — 738, 739
> Back leg and back ear — 434, 435
> Lower half of body — 434, 435, 436, 738
> Upper half of body — 3022, 434, 435, 436, 738

4. The tail is worked in Turkey knots using two strands of thread. Start at the upper edge of the tail and following the outline as shown, work rows of knots gradually shading from dark to light (434, 435, 436, 738). Using very sharp scissors and the eyebrow comb, cut and sculpt the squirrel's tail.

5. To complete the squirrel, work the nose and claws in straight stitches with one strand of dark brown thread (3371). Stitch a black petite bead in place for the eye, and a bronze bead at the end of the paws for the nut.

There are countless numbers of embroidery stitches, often with variations in name and methods of working. This glossary contains all the stitches used in this book and describes how the stitches have been worked for these projects. For ease of explanation, some of the stitches have been illustrated with the needle entering and leaving the fabric in the same movement. When working in a hoop this is difficult (or should be if your fabric is tight enough!), so the stitches have to be worked with a stabbing motion, in several stages.

The stitches are listed alphabetically for ease of reference.

Backstitch

This is a useful stitch for outlining a shape, e.g. the bee body. Bring the needle out at 1, insert at 2 (in the hole made by the preceding stitch) and out again at 3. Keep the stitches small and even.

Backstitch — Split

This is an easier version of split stitch, especially when using one strand of thread. Commence with a backstitch. Bring the needle out at 1, insert at 2 (splitting the preceding stitch) and out again at 3. This results in a fine, smooth line, ideal for stitching intricate curves.

Bullion Knots

These require some practice to work in a hoop. Use a straw needle of the appropriate size, with the number of wraps depending on the length of the knot required, e.g. the hedge-

hog's spines. Bring the needle out at 1, insert at 2 leaving a long loop. Emerge at 1 again (not pulling the needle through yet) and wrap the thread around the needle the required number of times. Hold the wraps gently between the thumb and index finger of the left hand while pulling the needle through with the right hand. Pull quite firmly and insert again at 2, stroking the wraps into place.

Buttonhole Stitch

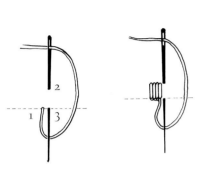

These stitches can be worked close together or slightly apart. Working from left to right, bring the needle out on the line to be worked at 1 and insert at 2, holding the loop of thread with the left thumb. Bring the needle up on the line to be worked at 3 (directly below 2), over the thread loop and pull through to form a looped edge. If the stitch is shortened and worked close together over wire, it forms a secure edge for cut shapes, e.g. a detached leaf.

Buttonhole Stitch — Long and Short

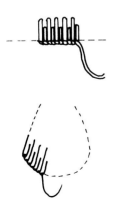

In long and short buttonhole stitch, each alternate stitch is shorter. If using the stitch to give a ruffled edge to flower petals, a better shape is achieved if the stitch is commenced above the edge. Bring the needle out at 1, insert at 2 and up again at 3 (like an open detached chain stitch). When embroidering a petal, angle the stitches towards the centre of the flower.

BUTTONHOLE WHEEL

This is buttonhole stitch worked in a circle, each stitch entering the material through the same central hole, e.g. the owl's eyes. An easy way to start is with a detached chain stitch from the central hole to the outside edge of the circle.

DETACHED BUTTONHOLE STITCH

Buttonhole stitch can be worked as a detached filling, attached only to the background material at the edges of the shape. First work a row of backstitches around the shape to be filled. Change to a fine tapestry needle. Bring the needle out at 1, work buttonhole stitches in to the top row of backstitches then insert the needle at 2. Come up again at 3 and work a buttonhole stitch into each loop of the preceding row. Insert the needle at 4. Quite different effects can be achieved when these stitches are worked close together or spaced apart.

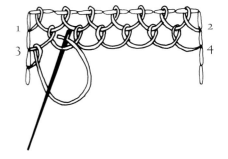

Detached buttonhole stitch can also be worked in circular form as a spiral, starting either from the outside edge or the centre.

This stitch can be used as a filling for a detached wired shape. Cover the wire with a foundation of buttonhole stitches to form the edge into which the detached filling is worked.

CORDED DETACHED BUTTONHOLE STITCH

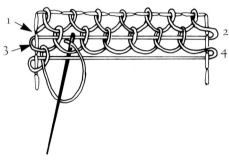

Detached buttonhole stitch can be worked over a laid thread. Outline the shape to be filled with backstitches. Using a tapestry needle, come up at 1 and work the first row of buttonhole stitches into the top row of backstitches. Slip the needle under the backstitch at 2. Take the needle straight back to the left side and slip under the backstitch at 3. Work another row of buttonhole stitches, this time taking the needle into the previous loops and under the straight thread at the same time. Slip the needle under the backstitch at 4 and continue as above.

To obtain a neater edge, the needle can be taken through to the back of the work at the end of each row (instead of under the backstitches), if preferred, e.g. the cornflower base. A contrasting thread (or gold thread), worked in another needle, can replace the straight thread, with interesting results.

Corded detached buttonhole stitch can also be used as a filling for a detached wired shape, e.g. the beetle wings.

CHAIN STITCH

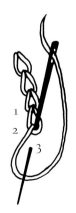

Can be used as an outline or filling stitch. Bring the needle through at 1 and insert it again through the same hole, holding the loop of thread with the left thumb. Bring the needle up a short distance along at 2, through the loop, and pull the thread through. Insert the needle into the same hole at 2 (inside the loop) and make a second loop, hold, and come up at 3. Repeat to work a row of chain stitch, securing the final loop with a small straight stitch.

CHAIN STITCH — DETACHED

Detached chain stitch, also known as Lazy Daisy Stitch, is worked in the same way as chain stitch except that each loop is secured individually with a small straight stitch. The securing stitch can be made longer if desired, to form sepals or thorns for roses. Different effects can be achieved by working several detached chain stitches inside each other.

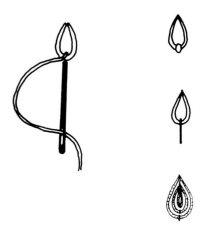

CHAIN STITCH — INTERLACED

This stitch, when interlaced with gold thread, forms a very pretty braid.

Work a row of chain stitch as a foundation, with two or three strands of thread. Interlace each side of this chain stitch with gold thread in a tapestry needle, as follows:

(1)   Come out at 1, slide the needle under the second chain at 2.

(2)   Slide the needle under both the first chain and interlacing thread at 3.

(3)   Slide the needle under the next chain at 4.

(4)   Slide the needle under both the chain and interlacing thread at 5.

(5)   Repeat the last two steps to the end of the row. Take the thread to the back of the work at the end of the last chain and secure.

Interlace the other side of the row of chain stitch. Bring the needle out at 1 and work as above, reversing the direction of the needle.

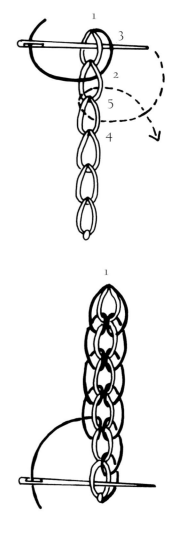

CHAIN STITCH — WHIPPED

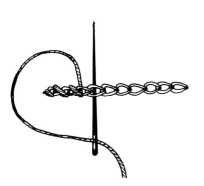

This is a useful method for working slightly raised outlines. Work a row of chain stitch, then bring the needle out slightly to one side of the final securing stitch. Using either the eye of the needle or a tapestry needle, whip the chain stitches by passing the needle under each chain loop from right to left, back to the beginning of the row. A contrasting (or gold) thread can be used for the whipping. When whipped chain stitch is used for stems, the thickness of the outline can be varied by the number of threads used.

COUCHING

Couching, with tiny upright stitches worked at regular intervals, is a way of attaching a thread, or group of threads, to a background fabric. The laid thread is often thicker or more fragile (e.g. gold or chenille) than the one used for stitching, and other types of stitches can be used to couch the threads e.g. buttonhole stitch. Couching stitches are also used for attaching wire to the base fabric before embroidering detached shapes.

FEATHER STITCH

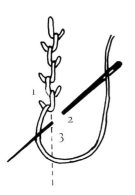

This stitch is made up of a series of loops, stitched alternately to the right and to the left, each one holding the previous loop in place. Come up on the line to be followed at 1. Insert the needle to the right at 2 and come up on the line again at 3, holding the thread under the needle with the left thumb. Repeat on the left side of the line, reversing the needle direction, e.g. veins for the gooseberry.

FEATHER STITCH — SINGLE

Work the feather stitch loops in one direction only to give a feathered outline to a shape, e.g. a rose leaf.

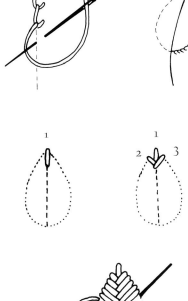

FISHBONE STITCH

This stitch is useful for filling small leaf shapes. Bring the thread out at the tip of the leaf 1, and make a small straight stitch along the centre line (vein). Bring the needle out at 2, make a slanted stitch and go down on the right of the centre line. Bring the needle out at 3, make a slanted stitch and go down on the left of the centre line, overlapping the base of the previous stitch. Continue working slanted stitches alternately from the left and the right, close together, until the shape is filled.

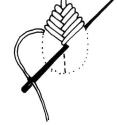

FLY STITCH

Fly stitch is actually an open detached chain stitch. Bring the needle out at 1 and insert at 2, holding the working thread with the left thumb. Bring up again at 3 and pull through over the loop. Secure the loop with an anchoring stitch which can vary in length to produce different effects, e.g. a short tie-down stitch is used for antennae. When working a row of vertical fly stitches, a longer tie-down stitch is required.

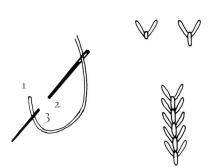

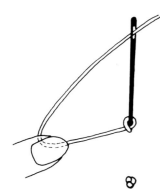

FRENCH KNOTS

Using a straw needle, bring the thread through at the desired place, wrap the thread once around the point of the needle and re-insert the needle. Tighten the thread and *hold taut* while pulling the needle through. To increase the size of the knot use more strands of thread, although more wraps can be made if desired.

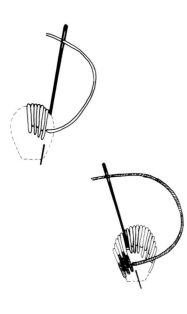

LONG AND SHORT STITCH

This stitch can be used to fill areas too large or irregular for satin stitch, or where shading is required. The first row, worked around the outline, consists of alternating long and short satin stitches. In the subsequent rows, the stitches are all of similar length, and fit into the spaces left by the preceding row. For a more realistic result when working petals, direct the stitches towards the centre of the flower. The surface will look smoother if the needle either pierces the stitches of the preceding row or enters at an angle between the stitches.

Scrap thread

NEEDLEWEAVING

Needleweaving is a form of embroidery where thread in a tapestry needle is woven in and out over two or more threads attached to the background fabric. Work needleweaving over a loop to form sepals e.g. dandelions. Use a length of scrap thread to keep the loop taut while weaving.

OVERCAST STITCH

This stitch is made up of tiny, upright satin stitches, worked very close together over a laid thread or wire, resulting in a firm raised line. When worked over wire it gives a smooth, secure edge for cut shapes, e.g. bees wings. Place the wire along the line to be covered. Working from left to right with a stabbing motion, cover the wire with small straight stitches, pulling the thread firmly so that there are no loose stitches which may be snipped when the shape is cut out. As cut shapes are fragile, ensure that the maximum amount of fabric is caught by the stitch, by holding the needle at right angles to the wire when piercing the fabric.

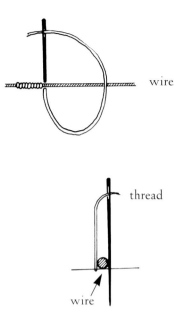

wire

thread

wire

PAD STITCH

Pad stitch is used as a foundation under satin stitch when a smooth, slightly raised surface is required. Padding stitches can be either straight stitches or chain stitches, worked in the opposite direction to the satin stitches. Felt can replace pad stitch for a more raised effect.

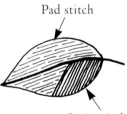

Pad stitch

Satin stitch

PALESTRINA KNOT STITCH

This stitch is also known as Double Knot Stitch. It makes a beautiful textured line or can be used to join two edges together decoratively, as in the stumpwork chatelaine.

Working from left to right, bring the needle out on the line to be covered, or edges to be joined. Make a small slanting stitch to the right (inserting the needle at right angles to the line), going down at 2 and coming up at 3. Pull the thread

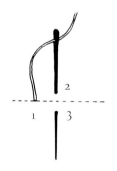

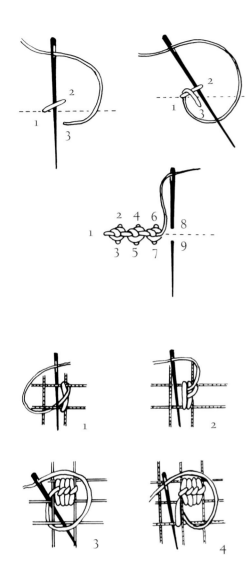

through then slide the needle, from above, under the stitch just made. Pull through then hold the thread below the stitch with the thumb. Coming from above, slip the needle under the first stitch again, to the right of the previous thread, bringing the needle through *over* the held thread (as in button-hole stitch).

Make the next slanting stitch to the right and continue as above, working the knots fairly close together. Experiment with threads, tension and spacing for different effects.

Rococo Stitch

Rococo stitch is a counted thread stitch very popular in the seventeenth century. It consists of diamond shaped bundles of stitches drawn together with holes between each bundle — the tighter the stitches are pulled the lacier the result. Rococo stitch is used on single canvas or wide-meshed double canvas, and is most easily worked in diagonal rows from the top right to bottom left of the area to be embroidered. Each bundle consists of four vertical stitches, worked over two canvas

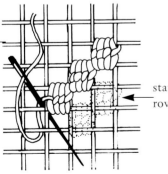

start next row here

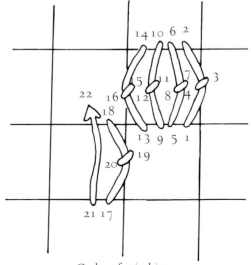

Order of stitching

threads, sharing the same holes at the top and bottom. Each of these vertical stitches is tied with a small horizontal stitch worked from right to left. The two outside vertical stitches are tied to the canvas with these horizontal stitches. Experiment with thread, canvas and tension with this stitch as a variety of effects can be achieved. When properly worked, no canvas background should remain showing. The diagrams show the order of stitching and the starting point for the next bundle.

ROUMANIAN COUCHING

This form of couching is useful for filling in large spaces.

Bring the needle out on the left, take a long stitch across the space to be filled then insert the needle on the right. This laid thread is then caught down with loose, slanting, couching stitches going from right to left. Traditionally the couching was worked with the same thread, however, a contrasting thread in another needle is very effective

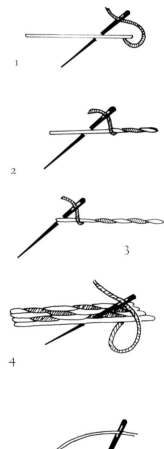

SATIN STITCH

Satin stitch is used to fill shapes such as petals or leaves. It consists of horizontal, vertical or slanted straight stitches, worked close enough together so that no fabric shows through, yet not overlapping each other. Satin stitch can be worked over a padding of felt or pad stitches and a smooth edge is easier to obtain if the shape is first outlined with split backstitch. When working a shaped area such as the poppy seed pod, work the centre stitch first then fill the shape with long stitches angled towards the stem for a realistic, rounded effect.

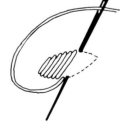

SATIN STITCH —
ENCROACHING

Encroaching satin stitch is a useful method of shading, as in the second and all subsequent rows, the head of each stitch is taken between the base of two stitches in the row above so that the rows blend softly into each other, e.g. the wings of the Blue butterfly.

SLIP STITCH

Slip stitch is a dressmaking stitch, used to join two folds of fabric together, invisibly, with small running stitches. The stitches are of equal length and enter and leave each fold of fabric directly opposite each other. Come out at 1, enter at 2, slide the needle through the fold and come out at 3, enter at 4 and so on, pulling the thread to bring the folds of fabric together. This stitch is used to join the front and back together in the Stumpwork Name Brooch.

STAB STITCH

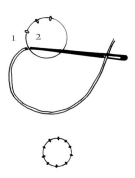

Stab stitch is used to apply a detached fabric shape, or felt, to the main fabric. It consists of small straight stitches made from the main fabric into the applied fabric, e.g. the owl or layers of felt for padding. Bring the needle out at 1, and insert at 2, catching in the edge of the applied piece.

STEM STITCH

Worked from left to right, the stitches in stem stitch overlap each other to form a fine line suitable for outlines and stems. To start, bring the needle out at 1 on the line to be worked. Go down at 2, come up at 3 and pull the thread through. Insert the needle at 4, holding the thread underneath the line with the left thumb, and come up again at 2 (in the same hole made by the previous stitch) then pull the thread through. Go down at 5, hold the loop and come up again at 4, then pull the thread through. Repeat to work a narrow line. If the stem stitches are worked at a slight angle a broader outline is formed, e.g. the leaves of the cornflowers.

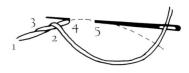

STEM STITCH — FILLING

Rows of stem stitch can be worked close together, following an outline, to form a very effective filling stitch. It is an ideal method for embroidering detached leaves, the rows of stem stitch being worked inside the wire outline, e.g. the leaves of the Oriental poppy.

STEM STITCH BAND — RAISED

Stem stitch can be worked over a foundation of straight stitches to form a detached filling. When this foundation of stitches is applied over lengths of padding thread, a raised, smooth, stem stitch band can be worked, ideal for branches and insect bodies. Lay a preliminary foundation of padding stitches worked with soft cotton thread. Across this padding,

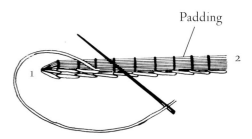

Padding

at fairly regular intervals, work straight stitches at right angles to the padding thread (do not make these stitches too tight). Then proceed to cover the padding by working rows of stem stitch over these straight stitches, using a tapestry needle so as not to pierce the padding thread. All the rows of stem stitch are worked in the same direction, close together and ending either at the same point, e.g. 1, or spaced as in satin stitch, e.g. 2.

STRAIGHT STITCH

Individual straight stitches, of equal or varying length, can be stitched with a variety of threads to achieve interesting effects, e.g. the rays on pansy petals in variegated thread.

TACKING (BASTING)

Tacking, a dressmaking term, is a row of running stitches, longer on the top of the fabric, used to temporarily mark an outline or to hold two pieces of fabric together.

TRELLIS STITCH

Trellis stitch, popular in the seventeenth century, is a needlelace filling stitch, attached only at the edges, and is most easily worked with a twisted silk thread. The first row of trellis stitch is worked into a foundation of backstitches, the size depending on the effect desired — close together and the trellis stitches resemble tent stitches in canvas work, further apart and an open trellis is the result.

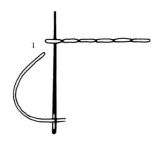

Bring the needle out at 1, slip it under the first backstitch (forming a t — a good way to remember this stitch), pull the thread through holding the resulting loop with the left thumb. Slip the needle through this loop (2) then pull the thread down, forming a firm knot. Repeat, to work a row of firm knots with loops in between. Insert the needle into the fabric at the end of the row.

To work a second row, bring the needle out at 3 and slip the needle through the loop between two knots, pull the thread through holding the resulting loop with the left thumb. Slip the needle through this loop (4) then pull the thread down, forming a firm knot. Repeat to the end of the row, insert the needle and continue as above.

The knots formed in trellis stitch are slanted in the direction the row is worked. When rows are worked in alternate directions the knots form a zig zag pattern, ideal for strawberries. When worked only in one direction the result is parallel slanting lines, e.g. the base of the acorn.

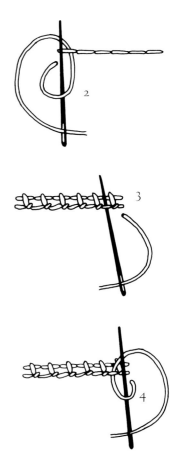

TURKEY KNOTS

Turkey knots are worked then cut to produce a soft velvety pile, e.g. for cornflower heads. Although there are several ways to work Turkey knots, the following method works well for small areas such as the bee's body. Use two strands of thread in a Number 9 crewel or straw needle.

Insert the needle into the fabric at 1 and pull through, holding a 5 cm (2'') tail with the left thumb. Come out at 2 and go down at 3 to make a small securing stitch. Bring the needle out again at 1 (can pierce the securing stitch), pull the thread down to form the second tail and hold with the left thumb.

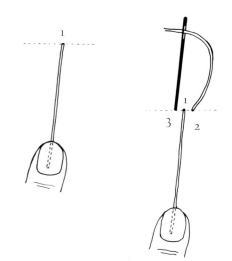

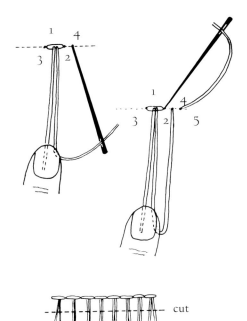

For the second Turkey knot, insert the needle at 4, still holding the tail. Come out at 5 and go down at 2 to make a small securing stitch. Bring the needle out again at 4, pull the thread down and hold with the left thumb as before. Repeat to work a row.

Work each successive row directly above the previous row, holding all the resulting tails with the left thumb. To complete, cut all the loops, comb with an eyebrow comb, and cut the pile to the desired length. The more the pile is combed the fluffier it becomes. The rows can be worked in alternate directions or all in one direction, and the density of the resulting pile depends on the number of stitches and rows worked in the area.

Whipped Spider Web Stitch

Whipped spider stitch is a form of needleweaving worked over a grid of foundation threads, which can be used to fill many different shapes, e.g. the carnation. First lay the foundation stitches, usually in a heavier thread, over the shape to be worked (this can be padded if required). Working from right to left, whip each of these laid threads with a backstitch, using a tapestry needle so as not to pierce the threads or the background fabric. Bring the needle out at the edge of the shape and slide under thread 1. Work a backstitch over 1 then slide the needle under thread 2. Work a backstitch over 2 then slide the needle under thread 3. Work a backstitch over 3 then insert the needle at the edge of the shape. Repeat, always working in the same direction, until the shape is filled, resulting in whipped ribs on the surface.

To work a circular, raised, whipped spider web lay four
long foundation stitches, as shown, securing the thread at the
back of the work. Gather and tie all these threads together in
the centre with a temporary length of thread. Using a tapestry
needle, bring the working thread up between these threads
and start whipping the spokes, working in a clockwise direction and pulling on the temporary thread at the same time,
causing the web to be raised in the middle. Continue, working back over one strand and forward under two until the
spokes are filled to the required amount, then remove the
spare thread, e.g. the centre of the Oriental poppy.

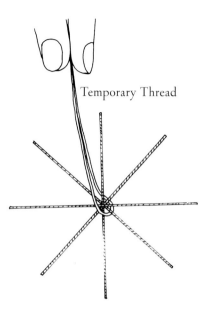

Temporary Thread

Temporary thread not
shown for clarity

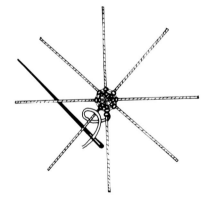

Thread Conversion Information

I have used DMC stranded cotton to embroider these designs unless otherwise specified. Other threads have been used for their qualities of lustre, colour or variegation when required. As some of these threads may not be readily available in other countries, a description and the nearest DMC equivalent or substitute is provided.

Au Ver à Soie d'Alger: 100% pure silk, spun — 7 strands, moderate lustre, floss weight, made in France.

SOIE D'ALGER	DMC
611	741
612	740
616	919
645	721
646	720/900
1316	327
1336 (bright purple)	No match
1343	340
1344	3746
1345	333
2125	469
2126	937
2132	3012
2134	3011
2926	814
2933	335
3024	3350
3322	3743
3323	3042
3326 (midnight purple)	No match / 939
3336	550
4636	902
4643	778
4644	3726
4645	3802

Madeira Silk: 100% pure silk, spun — 4 strands, moderate lustre, floss weight, made in Germany.

MADEIRA SILK	DMC
113	743
114	742
210	666/349
903	333
1714	317
2307	3825
Black	310
White	blanc

Cifonda Art Silk: fine, spun — 6 strands, high lustre, made in India. (Similar to Rajmahal).

CIFONDA	DMC
102	402
123	522
125	550
174	741
181	794
212	415
214	414
215	930
222	435
496	3033
497	612
498	610
1115	726
1116	725
Black	310

Minnamurra Cotton: hand-dyed, spun — 6 strands, floss weight, made in Australia. Each skein combines two or more colours which overlap and blend.

MINNAMURRA	DMC
110 (mauve blended to yellow)	552 ›‹ 3820

Bibliography and Further Reading

Baker, Muriel. *Stumpwork: The Art of Raised Embroidery*, Charles Scribner's Sons, New York, 1978.

Beck, Thomasina. *Embroidered Gardens*, Angus and Robertson, Sydney, 1979.

Beck, Thomasina. *The Embroiderer's Garden*, UK: David and Charles, 1988.

Beck, Thomasina. *The Embroiderer's Flowers*, David and Charles, UK, 1992.

Beck, Thomasina. *The Embroiderer's Story*, David and Charles, UK, 1995.

Best, Muriel. *Stumpwork: Historical and Contemporary Raised Embroidery*, Batsford, London, 1987.

Brooke, Xanthe. *Catalogue of Embroideries*, Alan Sutton, UK, 1992.

Brown, Walter R. *The Stuart Legacy: English Art 1603-1714*, Birmingham Museum of Art, USA, 1991.

Christie, Grace. *Embroidery and Tapestry Weaving*, Pitman, London, 1906.

Christie, Grace. *Samplers and Stitches*, Batsford, London, 1920.

Clabburn, Pamela. *The Needleworker's Dictionary*, Macmillan, UK, 1976.

Davis, Mildred J. *The Art of Crewel Embroidery*, Vista Books, London, 1962.

Don, Sarah. *Traditional Embroidered Animals*, David and Charles, UK, 1990.

Enthoven, Jacqueline. *The Stitches of Creative Embroidery*, Schiffer, USA, 1987.

Hillier, Malcolm. *Flowers*, Dorling Kindersley, London, 1988.

Hirst, Barbara and Roy. *Raised Embroidery*, Merehurst, London, 1993.

Hirst, Barbara and Roy. *New Designs in Raised Embroidery*, Merehurst, London, 1997.

Hughes, Therle. *English Domestic Needlework 1660 - 1860*, Abbey Fine Arts, London.

Huish, Marcus. *Samplers and Tapestry Embroideries*, Longmans Green, London, 1913.

Isaacs, Jennifer. *The Secret Meaning of Flowers*, Simon and Schuster, Australia, 1993.

King, Donald, and Levey, Santina. *Embroidery in Britain from 1200 to 1750*, Victoria and Albert Museum, London, 1993.

Lilley, E. and Midgley, W. *Studies in Plant Form and Design*, Chapman and Hall, London, 1916.

Morse, Richard. *The Book of Wildflowers*, Collins. London.

Nahmad, Claire. *Garden Spells*, Pavilion Books, London, 1994.

Pickles, Sheila. *The Language of Wild Flowers*, Pavilion Books, London, 1995.

Snook, Barbara. *English Embroidery*, Batsford, London, 1960.

Speirs, Gill, and Quemby, Sigrid. *A Treasury of Embroidery Designs*, Bell and Hyman, London, 1985.

Swain, Margaret. *Historical Needlework*, Barrie and Jenkins, UK, 1970.

Swain, Margaret. *Embroidered Stuart Pictures*, Shire Album, UK, 1990.

Thomas, Mary. *Dictionary of Embroidery Stitches*, Hodder and Stoughton, London, 1934.

Ware, Dora, and Stafford, Maureen. *An Illustrated Dictionary of Ornament*, Allen & Unwin, London, 1974.

Wilson, Erica. *Embroidery Book*, Charles Scribner's Sons, New York, 1973.

Index

Stumpwork Supplies and Kit Information

The threads, beads, brooches etc. referred to in this book (Au Ver à Soie d'Alger, Cifonda, DMC, Framecraft, Kreinik, Madeira, Mill Hill, Minnamurra, Needle Necessities) are available from specialist needlework shops.

All materials required for the projects may be obtained either in kit form or individually from Chelsea Fabrics. A Mail Order Service is available. Please write or telephone for information and price list.

CHELSEA FABRICS,

277 Bong Bong Street,

(P.O. Box 300)

BOWRAL. N.S.W. 2576.

AUSTRALIA.

Telephone: 02 48 611 175

Jane Nicholas discovered stumpwork in 1982 and since then has been engrossed in researching, doing and teaching this form of embroidery. Her first book, *Stumpwork Embroidery: A Collection of Fruits, Flowers and Insects for Raised Contemporary Embroidery*, was published in 1995 and her work has been featured in *Textile Fibre Forum* (1992), *Australian Country Craft and Decorating* (1994), the *Country Craft Collection Needlecraft* (1994), Popular Needlecraft (1995), *Embroidery and Cross Stitch* (1996), *Inspirations* (1997). Drawing on her background as a secondary school teacher, she has taught stumpwork throughout Australia for the past five years, and  more recently in the United States and New Zealand. She has taught at the Embroiderers' Guild of America National Seminar and has been invited to teach for the Canadian Embroiderers' Guild. Jane is an avid collector of old textiles, embroideries, buttons and needlework tools. She is married and has three children. She lives in Bowral, New South Wales, Australia.